Ninja Secrets
from the
Grandmaster

G000163018

Ninja Secrets
from the
Grandmaster

DR. MASAAKI HATSUMI
AND STEPHEN K. HAYES

CONTEMPORARY
BOOKS, INC.
CHICAGO ▪ NEW YORK

Library of Congress Cataloging-in-Publication Data

Hatsumi, Masaaki, 1931–
    Ninja secrets from the grandmaster.

    1. Hand-to-hand fighting, Oriental.   2. Ninjutsu.
I. Hayes, Stephen K.   II. Title.
U167.5.H3H36   1987   355.5'48   87-20090
ISBN 0-8092-5329-1

Copyright © 1987 by Stephen K. Hayes
All rights reserved
Published by Contemporary Books, Inc.
180 North Michigan Avenue, Chicago, Illinois 60601
Manufactured in the United States of America
Library of Congress Catalog Card Number: 87-20090
International Standard Book Number: 0-8092-5329-1

Published simultaneously in Canada by Beaverbooks, Ltd.
195 Allstate Parkway, Valleywood Business Park
Markham, Ontario L3R 4T8 Canada

This book is dedicated to the memory of
the divine warrior
Toshitsugu Takamatsu
Moko no Tora

CONTENTS

AUTHOR'S INTRODUCTIONS

Last year, I visited America twice. I spoke with many people there who are confused and bewildered by all the misconstrued and fallacious ideas that unfortunately have become a part of the 1980s ninja boom. In my personal appearances, I used my heart and body to guide my American friends to the truth of the essence of the ninja's art. My statement was that only that person with a truly benevolent heart dedicated to justice could possibly be considered an authentic ninja. I constantly remind my students that it is a twisted and improper interpretation of the ninja's code of living to directly interfere with or cause difficulty for other people or the great cosmic natural scheme.

Therefore, I explained to the people in America that the reason I came was not to sell my name. I feel that it goes without saying that I made my trips to the United States because I wanted to correct the misinterpretations fostered by the ninja boom. My purpose was to assist people to know the heart and techniques of true ninjutsu, and thereby spread the knowledge correctly. This was my way of contributing to the happiness of the American people.

The historical ninja's extremely valuable methods were born from a blend of living their philosophy consistently and producing solutions to problems spontaneously. Through this pragmatic application of creative thought, they were able to survive an age of endless battles and to realize eventual enlightenment. We now live in an age of peace today, but we nevertheless continue to encounter difficulties in our daily lives. My own teachings are based on those methods employed by the ninja to survive this past thousand years, and are just as valid in the pursuit of happiness today as they were a millenium ago.

I have always taught through direct example, but it is true that the number of people who can participate directly in my seminars is but a small percentage of the world's population. For that reason, I have chosen to express my feelings and thoughts to a wider audience through the publication of this volume. By means of the interviews contained herein, I hope to share my *shinobigatari*, or "ninja communication," to assist the world in understanding and seeing the value in the ninja's way of thinking and viewing things.

March 10, 1987
Toratsugu
(Masaaki Hatsumi)

Over twenty years ago, I first read of the legendary Japanese warrior wizards known as the ninja. I was at once captivated by the power and allure of the image of these phantom combatives, said to be able to accomplish their desires through the strength of their will alone. I lamented the fact that I had been born on the wrong side of the Pacific and in the wrong nation and culture, for in the lore of the ninja I found reflected the secret bent of my own heart.

Not in my wildest dreams did I then suspect that there might ever arrive a day when the grandmaster of the ninja would request that I co-author a book with him for the purpose of stating his personal views on the history and significance of the art of ninjutsu. Let this volume then stand as a testament to the power of the will, and may it serve to inspire all who are courageous enough to dare to transform their childhood dreams into reality.

March 10, 1987
Kinryu
(Stephen K. Hayes)

Authors Masaaki Hatsumi and Stephen K. Hayes.

Ninja Secrets
from the
Grandmaster

1
HERITAGE

Rumiko and I walk through pleasantly chilly Noda City, Chiba Prefecture, on our way to the conference office of ninjutsu grandmaster Masaaki Hatsumi. Octobers in Japan are always warmer than those in our midwestern American home, and light winds move gray clouds about behind and above the reds, golds, and browns of the foliage that still clings to the few trees in this small industrial city best known for its sprawling soy sauce factories. We move through the traffic of the small narrow streets, a whir of moving bodies, ringing bicycle warning bells, and straining automobile engines. The familiar and yet still somewhat exotic sights and sounds and smells of Japan envelope me. It is good to be back again.

I haven't seen Rumiko for over a month. She and our daughters had jetted their way to Japan two weeks after I had left them in America. I had departed earlier, bound in my solitary pilgrimage for China, Tibet, Nepal, and India. I had arrived just last night at Narita's Tokyo International Airport on an Air India flight from New Delhi, and taken a taxi across the sleeping Chiba Prefecture countryside to darkened Noda City, where I had been reunited with my waiting wife.

We walk through the grounds of the lovely, weathered old Atago Jinja, central shrine in the middle of Noda City's tiny business center district. A few tall trees loom overhead and shade the dark wood of the main shrine and its attendant outbuildings. Huge intricately carved wooden dragons, wiry and ageless, curl up the sides of the shrine structure as pillars and wriggle out from beneath the gray tiles as roofing structure supports. A tiny girl barely three is dressed in a marvelously colorful kimono, sashes and silk panels a wild and flowered swirl of oranges, pinks, greens, and sky blues. Her parents pose her before the shrine steps for a photograph. Dutifully serious, the miniscule beauty adopts a sideways stand and turns her head ever so slightly to catch the dim midmorning sun on her perfectly made-up face. She stares briefly at Rumiko and me, seemingly unaware of or unconcerned with my foreignness, and then turns her somber attention back to her coaching mother and father. I think of the daughters I have not seen for over one month.

The entire grounds of the Atago shrine are gravelled, save the stone walks that angle across the courtyard before the looming wooden structure. Massive granite lanterns ring the courtyard, tucked here and there among the grandfatherly old trees that somehow survived the paving and bulldozing and building that accompanied the postwar buildup of this small old city nestled here on the banks of the Edo River. In another decade I used to come to the shady environs of this comfortable timeless holy ground to sit and reflect, to write letters home, and to wait for the sundown that, in those days when I was too poor to afford a wristwatch, indicated that ninjutsu training would soon begin.

Down the streets past the rope sellers, carpet vendors, fruit peddlers, and incense shops, we walk. Bright blue plastic tubs full of squirming silver fish cascade water onto the street as the fish market's hoses pump fresh water into the small pools as they have for as long as I can remember. The captivating smell of stacked lumber reaches out to grab us as we continue down the main thoroughfare, bound for our meeting with Masaaki Hatsumi, grandmaster of the ninja and our personal mentor in the Japanese arts of combat enlightenment.

On a side street, we come to the featureless gray three-story building that houses the *bettaku* (alternate home) of Dr. Hatsumi. Here, where there is more room to spare, the grandmaster often conducts his meetings, interviews, and informal teaching sessions.

It was often joked among the students that the doctor had already filled up one home with a lifetime's collection of books and albums, antiques, weapons, curios, animals and cages, and souvenirs donated by visitors from around the world. He was now working on a second such collection, the humorous rumor had it. Would there someday be a third such dwelling, filled with the souvenirs of another lifetime's worth as the eccentric grandmaster of the ninja continued on through his days?

Dr. Hatsumi rounds the corner in his usual jaunty gait. His legs shuffle quickly, dragging the backs of his slip-on sandals along the paving of the side street. His whole body moves as a flowing unit, hands and arms swinging and head scanning in all directions. His right swinging arm continues its arc to lift and become a sort of informal salute as his face locks on us and beams into an ear-to-ear smile. He calls out in greeting from the end of the street. Ironically, as I am bowing to my teacher in Japanese fashion he saunters up and with another swinging salute pats me American-style roughly on the shoulder several times.

It is good to be back.

Rumiko, the grandmaster, and I take the stairs and enter the apartment that serves as the sensei's alternate home and office. He is moving and speaking in an extremely casual manner, as though we had last met yesterday, while it had in fact been three months since we had ridden together predawn in the silver limousine to the Dayton International Airport to see him off for Japan after his visit to our home in Ohio. Our last sight of the grandmaster of the ninja had been in the departure corridor of the airport, where he had insisted on continuing to instruct us in the ninja's *kuji no ho* (spiritual protection method) and *shinobitanto* (knife-fighting skills) until, at the last possible moment, we forced him onto the waiting aircraft.

The three of us sit now at the low table in the center of the main room and talk of recent events and travels, of health, our training, and our two daughters who now stay with their grandparents on the island of Kyushu. We sip pale green Japanese tea from handleless cups. We talk of old times and new, old challenges that were eventually converted into triumphs, and new confrontations that hopefully someday will produce similarly cheerful results.

The conversation turns to the effects the years have had on the form taken by my training with the grandmaster. In the early years, it was all rough-and-tumble combat in the back room of

the doctor's home. Little needed to be said in those days when
every physical technique was a new revelation. Now, all the early
years of physically demanding combat preparation are tempered
with a balance of strategy, psychology, philosophy, and spiritual
work. This is the way his training with his own teacher had gone,
Masaaki Hatsumi tells me.

I comment to the grandmaster that I wish all the world's
ninjutsu enthusiasts could sit in on such a conversation. It would
help so much for them to see that just like the skills of ninjutsu
themselves, the training methods as well continue to evolve as the
practitioner grows in terms of experience and personal insight.
Unfortunately, there is now so very much misunderstanding as to
what the true essence of the ninja art really is. There is even more
confusion in the martial arts world as to just who should be
listened to and who should be ignored when it comes to authority
to speak about the *shinobi* realm.

Hatsumi-sensei leaps to his feet. He darts to a tall narrow closet
built into the wall. Without a word, he proceeds to sort through
several small boxes and travelling cases until he finds just what he
had been searching for. He returns to the table with a small
portable tape recorder and three fresh cassette tapes. The grandmaster inserts a tape, tests the volume of the microphone, and
then places the recorder on the table between us. With an air of
triumph, he stares across the table at me and speaks.

Masaaki Hatsumi (MH): This is an important conversation, too important to let go. Let's turn this into a book. The three of us can work on this book together as a means of getting the truth out to the world. I know your publisher Contemporary will handle it. The sooner this comes out the better. I think that this is much more important than any other book I could work on at this moment.

No matter what comes to mind, no matter how sensitive you might think it to be, if you have any thoughts, please speak up. There are so many Japanese things that people do not understand. If you do not understand, Hayes-san, that means that no one in America could possibly understand. You have been involved with this art for so many years, and still you might find some things that are yet a little unclear. I'm sure that there are many questions you might have. Ask me straightforwardly. I will answer, for the sake of the people of America, for the sake of the people of the world. In that sense, for this book you will represent all the martial artists of the world, Hayes-san. Anything at all, with nothing off-limits. I will give you my views.

Stephen K. Hayes (SKH): Well, just for the record, let's start with the beginning. How did you come to get involved in the martial arts in the first place?

MH: My reason for entering the world of martial arts had to do with survival in a violent world. My father was an alcoholic from my early years. When he was drunk, he would do things like find a blade in the kitchen, pick it up, and then become very violent. When I was little, I of course did not have the strength to disarm him or control him. I had to escape or hide to protect myself. It sounds strange, but I would just wake up naturally to hear my father's footsteps from very far away when he was drunk. I was that sensitive to danger as a small child. I would then conceal myself in a closet or any other place I could find to hide.

Since my childhood days, I have been living the art of ninjutsu, as taught through necessity by my father's actions. This was one of my motivations to get involved with the martial arts. I had to learn to control him and put him to bed. So I was living a technique called *shin ken shiraha dori* ("live sword white blade catching"). In that sense, it was my father who put me on this path. Therefore, I am thankful to my father. When he was not drunk, he was a wonderful person. That was a hardship I had to endure, and I eventually passed through that stage of my life.

When I first met Takamatsu-sensei, the feeling I got from him was not an impression of strength or weakness, or anything to do with skills. It was a feeling that could only be described as frightening or chilling.

I am so grateful to have been born into such circumstances to obtain this secret of the powers of *kuji* and *juji* (ninja spiritual powers). I feel that my students will never be able to understand the essential secrets of the *kuji* and *juji* methods unless they go through similar hardships. So for that reason, I do what I do in my role as teacher to my students.

SKH: Can you give us some of your first impressions of what it was like in the early days of training with your teacher Toshitsugu Takamatsu? At that time, could you even imagine how it would all turn out, who you were destined to become?

MH: Let me tell you the story of my involvement with Takamatsu-sensei from the beginning. He had spent years in China, and had been given the name *Moko no Tora* (Mongolian Tiger) while he was living there. I also understand that he was treated very well by the political leaders of China at that time. He took an active part in the martial arts community while he was in China. As I mentioned before, he was referred to as the Mongolian Tiger. He was just that strong. I met him when he was approaching seventy, and he died when he was over eighty years old. He was living in the Nara area when I was training with him all those years during the 1950s and 1960s.

A friend of his who knew of his activities in China said to him one time, "You were referred to as the Mongolian Tiger, but I think you look more like the Yamato Housecat." Yamato is the old name for the Nara region. Takamatsu-sensei replied, "Because I was able to transform myself from a tiger into a housecat, I have managed to live on to this advanced old age. Besides, everyone knows how much women like to cuddle housecats in their laps."

He said this with a laugh, of course. He was a very tough individual. Anyway, he was almost seventy years old when I met him.

SKH: You were in your mid-twenties when you met Toshitsugu Takamatsu, right? You already had a background in other Japanese martial arts at that time.

MH: Before I met Takamatsu-sensei, I had been involved with judo, karate, and aikido, as well as other Japanese martial arts, and I had teaching licenses in all these arts. When I was younger I was a much bigger man, and could get away with using my strength and size. I also studied various styles of *kobujutsu* (old Japanese weapons arts). At one time, I was spending between two- to three-hundred-thousand Yen (approximately $2,000) per month to learn a certain style of kobujutsu from a particular teacher.

SKH: I'll have to tell that story whenever any of my students whine about how much it costs them to study the art of ninjutsu in America.

Toshitsugu Takamatsu initiates his young student Masaaki Hatsumi in the applications of one of the ninja's *kuji-in* energy-channelling hand postures.

Toshitsugu Takamatsu, also known as the Mongolian Tiger, teacher of current grandmaster Masaaki Hatsumi. In the *yoko ichi-monji no kamae* staff fighting posture, the two downward-pointing fingers symbolize the point at which *in* and *yo* (negative and positive polarity charges) energies meet. From that point, the energy can vary and change freely, both avoiding and piercing as appropriate.

MH: The inability to handle financial pressures is one of the main reasons why so many people ultimately fail in the martial arts. If you are plagued by the difficulties of never having enough money to do what you need to do, buy the equipment you need to buy, or be where you need to be, you will never make it.

SKH: That's very interesting. A friend of mine, a teacher of Chinese martial arts, has this theory that in old China, only the wealthy could become truly proficient in the martial arts. The poor were so poor that every moment of time and every ounce of energy had to be devoted to earning enough money to survive. Only the wealthy had the time to study and train regularly. Also, only the wealthy had enough money to tempt any true master of the fighting arts to divulge what were in fact the precious survival secrets that had kept him alive while others had died.

MH: I have to say, though, that it was thanks to that expensive instructor that I came to know of Toshitsugu Takamatsu, the man who would eventually become my teacher.

Rumiko Hayes (RH): What was your first impression of Takamatsu-sensei?

MH: When I first met Takamatsu-sensei, the feeling I got from him was not an impression of strength or weakness, or anything to do with skills. It was a feeling that could only be described as frightening or chilling. It was just like the chant of the Shinto priest as he stands in front of the shrine and repeats, *"Kashikomi kashikomi mo san"* ("Awesome one, awesome one, I beseech you."). *Awesome* is the only word I can use. It was not at all a normal feeling. I found myself immobilized, frozen in place. It was as though something held me or covered me so that I could not move. I could only stare at the man. My impression was: "A martial artist like this man still exists in the world!"

One year before Takamatsu-sensei's death, I felt that I ought to take my students to meet him at least once, so I arranged to take them down to Nara with me to see him. They all felt the same way, that overwhelming impression of awe. Tetsuji Ishizuka even said that he too felt a chill go down his spine.

I have met many teachers of the various martial arts in my years, but meeting this warrior named Takamatsu was a unique experience. Even though I could see him standing there, it was as though he really was not there, as though he existed in some other dimension. Awesome, scary, creepy—these are the only words I can use to describe it. I had never felt that way at all with any other martial arts teachers I met.

I feel that the title of soke, *or "grandmaster" as you usually translate it, was in fact given to me way before my technique had matured. In a similar manner, I sometimes do the same thing to my students.*

From the time of our first encounter until the time he died, he taught me. The training was incredible, incredible, incredible.

RH: How do you mean that?

MH: For example, one cold evening he ordered me to follow him and bring a sword. He took the sword out of the scabbard and sprayed sake from his mouth onto the tip of the long blade. He commented on how cold it was that evening. It was indeed a bitter cold winter night, and the moon was shining down over the roof of Kashiwabara Shrine. We were walking along together and he suddenly said, "I am going to come at you with this sword." He grabbed the sword, a real one with a razor edge, and asked, "Are you ready?"

I told him I was.

The sword sliced down at me and I grabbed it. I didn't have any choice. If I had hesitated even in the slightest, I would have been cut open. It was the only thing I could do, grab it without hesitating.

RH: Your hand was not cut?

MH: No, not cut at all. I think the fact that Takamatsu-sensei was so good at cutting had a lot to do with it. But since I had been ordered to grab it, I grabbed it. That was the only thing of which I was aware. It was a cold winter night, and when I grabbed the sword with my cold hand, I remember the blade giving off a noise.

The sword was easy to grab. The spear was worse, the *fukuro yari* (short-pointed spear). Ah, those were the good old days, when I could get away with carrying a spear on the train in Japan! Takamatsu-sensei would order me to grab the spear as he attacked me with it. I grabbed it. That was all a part of the training I had to go through.

SKH: It is that kind of training, that experience of cultivating the power of intention, that is so difficult to get across in martial arts training in America. When things start to get challenging, I mean *really* challenging, so many students just back off.

MH: The *gokui* secret teachings of our Takagi Yoshin ryu tradition contain a story about catching a bee. There is a power phrase that goes *"Amo issun no tamamushi!"* By saying this mantra and grabbing a bee without hesitating, you will avoid being stung. Supposedly, when the bee is entirely covered, he looses his power to sting. In summation, what this really means is that the mantra reminds and encourages us to be fearless and unhesitating when we take action.

RH: Can we put this in the book? If it is a secret teaching, perhaps we should delete it from the tape.

MH: No, no, put it in the book. That's fine. The story is merely an illustration of the secret method that will of course not appear in the book for everyone to see.

SKH: I wonder how many readers will get themselves stung trying to test this half-a-technique.

MH: As I know you have heard already, one time Takamatsu-sensei told me to sit with my eyes closed while he left the room. I could not hear his footsteps as he returned, because he was a ninja, but I felt something awful. I moved my body and I could hear the noise of something slicing through the air. "What's that?! Is this some kind of test?" I wondered. I had heard about this from him before. I told myself not to panic, and sat back in position again.

A moment later, I felt that same strange sensation, so I flattened myself on the tatami. I could again hear the noise of the blade as it passed over my head. It turned out that he was cutting at me with a *juji* ("number 10," a cross-shaped letter character) pattern, one slice vertically and one slice horizontally. After that, I was awarded the title of *soke*.

SKH: Were you surprised to receive the grandmaster title, or was that something that you had expected?

MH: I feel that the title of *soke*, or "grandmaster" as you usually translate it, was in fact given to me way before my technique had matured. In a similar manner, I sometimes do the same thing to my students. Even though a person may not be qualified for a given rank technically, I give them the rank in order to pressure them into growing stronger in the future.

Takamatsu-sensei eventually died in the early 1970s, right before you came to Japan for the first time, Hayes-san. All those times I visited Takamatsu-sensei over those fifteen years, his wife always served me sake, but I never touched it. Now I tell this story to my students as they sip from a cup of sake I have served them. Sometimes I do feel a little bit bad about that! Anyway, as a part of the ceremony at his funeral, the *kiyome* purification ritual, I drank some sake. That was the first time I had ever drunk sake around my teacher. That was the level of the training.

I never felt that I was afraid of the training. I must have been drawn to rough or dangerous things like that by my inherent nature. I was brought up by my alcoholic father, so things like that, bold survival tactics, became a natural part of my personality. A feel for actual fighting was there in me already. Takamatsu-sensei once praised me by saying that he had never met anyone bolder than I. Boldness can also be seen as recklessness, as I have so often said before, so my so-called fearlessness could really be a form of foolishness. (Laughter.)

So that is the story of how I inherited the title of *soke*. Every time I went to Takamatsu-sensei's home in Kashiwabara, there was plenty of training.

RH: How long did it take in those days to go from Noda to Kashiwabara?

MH: It was a long way to go. I took a night train to arrive there in the morning. We would then put in a full day of training. I took the night train back, and arrived in the morning in time to open up my clinic. I did this for fifteen years. In the beginning I took a lot of notes and photos. But I could not actually perform all those things that I wrote down in my notebook. I felt bitter and angry in the beginning because I could not do the techniques I was being shown, even though I was an experienced martial arts teacher.

Whenever I went down to Kashiwabara, I wanted to get as many techniques as I could get, but I could not get anything right. It went on like that for two to three years. When Takamatsu-sensei eventually gave me some scrolls, he told me, "Writing things down is a foolish waste of energy." He said that to me several times, but it never really sank in. He said to me, "To write things down is a foolish waste. I know that, but if I leave something on paper, maybe somebody in the future will be able to rediscover something based on what I wrote. He may become a master. So I put some things down here after all and am handing these scrolls on to you."

I say the same thing to my students. When they get to certain skill levels, I tell them not to bother taking photos or writing

things down anymore. You understand that I am not doing that as a means of tricking anyone, of holding on to my techniques and keeping them all to myself. It's not a matter of stealing or of having stolen. I do not have to worry about that at all. My techniques evade even the video cameras.

After coming to that realization about the futility of literally preserving techniques, I gave up everything and just followed whatever Takamatsu-sensei taught. At the same time, I was in turn teaching whatever I learned to my students. That is what I call the Byakuryu ["White Dragon," the warrior name given to Masaaki Hatsumi by his teacher Toshitsugu Takamatsu] period. I was Byakuryu first and then later was called Byakuryuoh ("Venerable White Dragon"). The students who were studying with me at that time—you were included in that group too, Hayes-san— really deserve an apology. I hardly had any idea of what was going on myself, and yet I was claiming to be teaching you.

SKH: That's OK. I did the same thing to my early students, too.

MH: After Takamatsu-sensei's death, I trained on my own in this art for fifteen more years. And as I told you before, I feel like I have at last reached the full potential of my *soke* title. So the truth is: my art takes about five or ten years to figure out, once

I thought a long time about the importance of balance between religious study and martial arts practice. Your religion has to be the right one, a religion that leads to your becoming a better, stronger person.

you have been taught the fundamental techniques. Realizing this truth is a part of the subtle, exquisite beauty of the martial arts.

RH: Did Toshitsugu Takamatsu ever explain to you that the process would take that long?

MH: At one point, Takamatsu-sensei once-and-for-all told me that I would never be a *meijin*, a master of the martial arts. He said that I could become a *tatsujin*, or "completed human being." I was so disappointed to hear that. I thought that it must be that I did not have the talent required to reach master level. For a long time, Takamatsu-sensei did not tell me the meaning of *tatsujin*, as he used the term. But as I kept training in the art over the years, I thought about what he said about *meijin* and *tatsujin*. I finally came to realize just what a high compliment he had actually given me.

Tatsujin is in all an implication of becoming a total human being. How difficult it is to become a total human being! This was truly a supreme compliment, and now I regret my lack of perception at that time. To live as a human being, you do not need to be obsessed with who is strong and who is weak. If you are an animal, you have to be strong to survive in the animal realm of nature. But humans can live regardless of their outward strength. I think that is the wonderful aspect of the human fighting arts. That is the way I was taught by Takamatsu-sensei.

SKH: Did you continue to train actively with Takamatsu-sensei up to the time of his death?

MH: One year before his death, Takamatsu-sensei told me that he had taught me everything he knew. Everything. He said that since he had taught me all he had to teach, he had fulfilled his obligation to pass on the teachings of the lineages he had been given. He said that from that point on, he intended to devote all his time to spiritual training.

When my teacher told me that, I felt as though I had been

abandoned. It was the loneliest moment of my life. I felt as though I was not nearly good enough to be on my own.

It was intriguing though, that this battler was so interested in spiritual study. I thought a long time about the importance of balance between religious study and martial arts practice. Your religion has to be the right one, a religion that leads to your becoming a better, stronger person. So I suppose it is natural for your religion to change its form according to where you live. Religion, or *shukyo* in Japanese, is written with characters that mean "essential" and "teachings" for human beings. Very basic and very important teachings. Therefore, religion changes its form depending on where you live, whether it is cold or hot, prosperous or poor. Where people depend on the water, they are sure to create a god of water.

I was 27 years old when I met Takamatsu-sensei. When I think about it now, the phrase *bushido wa shinukoto to mitsuketari* ("bushido is the way of death"), comes to mind. It was as though I died when I was 27 years old. From childhood, for some reason, I had always felt a premonition that I would die at age 27. When I met Takamatsu-sensei, the previous Masaaki Hatsumi died at that moment. From that time on, there was no more Masaaki Hatsumi. Instead of me having my own life, I was given the 900-year-long life of our ancestors. That is how I regard the phrase, *bushido wa shinukoto to mitsuketari.* It has nothing to do with committing *seppuku* (ritual suicide for the sake of honor) or anything of that sort. I was given a place and an opportunity to die to all I had been previously. I was given that by Takamatsu-sensei. I died there when I was 27.

Therefore, I don't claim to have my own thoughts anymore. I guess that is part of the reason why I so often act on impulse, moment to moment. Since these cannot be called my own thoughts, I sometimes feel that I might give others a bad impression or that I might hurt somebody's feelings, though. But those who have been training in this art for a long time, when they reach a certain level, will understand me. I like to care for those people who are capable of making it to that certain level. Before they reach that level, I simply observe them.

I believe that is what the true *buyu* ("martial friend") concept is all about. If a person has the quality in him to be one of those who makes it through the training, he will be one of my *buyu*. I do not believe that everybody who enters my dojo will be able to make it all the way through to the higher levels of this art, so I do not feel any necessity to try to make everybody get this art. I never even attempt to try to make all the students understand.

Since I cannot do the impossible, I play. What I have now has developed to the level that cannot be taught. So you cannot be taught. You have to catch it for yourself. That's the only way. Avoiding the sword from behind as the *godan* test for fifth degree is an example of what I am talking about. I cannot teach a student how to pass it.

RH: We heard that you named your dojo *Bujinkan* ("divine warrior hall") after Takamatsu-sensei because you considered him the essence of the divine warrior. How about your teacher Toshitsugu Takamatsu? Did he have a dojo himself, and what did he call it?

MH: Yes, he did. But because of the war, and also because he ended up spending all those years in China, he did not pay much attention to running a formal training hall. Besides, judo and kendo were considered to be more fashionable in those days, and it was also true that history did not allow him to get the word around about what he had to teach. As I recall, I think his original training hall was referred to as *Sukisha*, or "(place for) people who enjoy (warrior arts training)." I heard he had many students when he was in China. He had several matches with strong martial artists in China, and he made a lot of martial friends there.

Toshitsugu Takamatsu, the 33rd grandmaster.

There are several stories about his days in China. Cho Shiro, a huge Chinese, engaged Takamatsu-sensei in a match for over an hour. Cho ended up out of breath, and Takamatsu thought that moment was his chance to win. Someone named Ren Keimei stopped the match right at that moment, before either man had scored a decisive victory over the other. But this Cho knew in his heart that he had lost, so he asked Takamatsu to be his friend and martial brother. It turned out that this Cho Shiro was the personal bodyguard of Cho Sakurin, the well-known Chinese political figure, and was later killed in the scandalous train explosion that took the life of Cho Sakurin in 1928. In China, Toshitsugu Takamatsu was called Moko no Tora.

SKH: Moko—that's Japanese for Mongolia?

MH: Yes, and also, if you write *Moko tora* in Japanese characters, it can also be written to mean "fierce old tiger." Everybody called him Moko tiger.

SKH: So Takamatsu-sensei gave you the name Byakuryu?

MH: Yes, that's right.

SKH: Was there a meaning, a significance behind that choice of name?

MH: Takamatsu-sensei told me that when he had to focus his intention on accomplishing something important, he used a technique whereby he visualized himself as a white dragon to facilitate making his goal become a reality. So he asked me, "How about White Dragon? Does it suit you? It is appropriate for you to have a *bugo* (martial name) now." So I was given the name Byakuryu as my martial name. And then when I reached a certain level, when he died, I became Byakuryuoh, taking one piece of the name from Takamatsu-sensei's name Uoh. I took the *oh* portion in honor of his memory. In Japanese, *oh* can also be written with the character that means "king," so in a sort of play on words, I can also think of Byakuryuoh as meaning "white dragon king," as well.

SKH: How did you know to alter your name? Is that a part of the lore that was taught to you by Toshitsugu Takamatsu?

MH: The reason why I altered my name to Byakuryuoh is a long and complex story. When I first met Takamatsu-sensei, he told me bluntly that I was as insignificant as an insect. He called me *mushikera* in a single-word dismissal. What an insult. But then he admonished me to train, holding in mind that I am a mere insect. "Even an insect," he told me, "if it holds on to a horse's tail, can go for thousands of miles. Therefore, you hold on, too."

When I was compared with an insect, I was very disappointed. I thought I must not be very good at all. Until then, I was full of confidence, but when I trained with Takamatsu-sensei, he threw me onto the ground in the same casual manner that he might have used to flick an insect onto the ground. One time he praised me, and at that time I came to think, even in the world of insects, there was a time when reptiles ruled the earth as kings. *Hachurui* is "reptile" in Japanese, and the kanji character for the *chu* in the middle of the word is the kanji for "insect."

Though I am referring to reptiles, Hayes-san, I'm not talking about iguanas here, as in Iguana kenpo. (Laughter.)

RH: Iguana kenpo?

SKH: It's a joke. Several years ago, I was commenting to Dr. Hatsumi that I had not been America's *only* ninja for very long. As soon as the magazines had begun to pay attention to me, all these phonies had popped up claiming that they too were ninjutsu masters. Of course none of them had ever appeared in any magazines until I had gotten the ninja ball rolling. Dr. Hatsumi said that we ought to make up some ridiculous art, something like the "iguana style." We could invent techniques where we hunch forward with our elbows angled up and have our tongues dart in and out as we swing our heads from side to side. We would then talk it up in the magazines. Then we could sit back and laugh at all the imposters who would of course pop up to claim violently that they were really the true masters of the legendary iguana method.

MH: So when Takamatsu-sensei died, I recalled the way I felt when I discovered that insect kanji there in the middle of the reptile king's name. And that is how I came to take the *oh*, meaning "king" as well as the literal "venerable" translation, as a part of my martial name.

SKH: Here is an amusing parallel. Years ago, when I had just moved to Japan to train with you, one of my Japanese friends visited the training hall in Noda City to watch our workout. When he asked how my training was going, you told him that no one in your dojo was doing well at all. You called the seniors "babes" in the art, and commented to him that I was so far below them that I could only be thought of as dust. (Laughter.) What a disappointment! Dust.

Well, I knew that *hokori*, the Japanese word you had used for dust, could also be written with a different character that sounded the same but meant "pride." I vowed that night that I would someday transform that *hokori* that meant dust on the floor of our ninja tradition into the *hokori* that meant pride of our tradition.

Meanwhile, I found Rumiko here who can help me keep this place dusted out. (Laughter.) And I suppose that someday I will have to add "dust" to whatever ninja name you end up giving me.

MH: Fifteen years have now passed since Takamatsu-sensei died. I am now called Toratsugu, and I finally feel that I am a full and true part of the current of the 900-year legacy. Because my title of soke was given to me before I was fully seasoned and matured as a warrior, I feel that I have to operate the same way when it comes to my students. I give out first- and second-degree ranks in the hopes that the student will someday fully embody what the rank title implies. I do that because I care about people.

SKH: Well, as I have so often brought up in our conversations, that policy really confuses the students in America and Europe. My belt-licensing policies for my students have to be different from those in Japan. The requirements for black belt ranks in my training halls are pretty tough. There is no way that I could get away with giving black belt ranks to my students in anything less than a manner that demands the total development of the individual. Any other way and I would be accused of selling ranks.

MH: I am not giving out these rank licenses for business purposes. Since most of these students have some sort of back-

Because my title of soke *was given to me before I was fully seasoned and matured as a warrior, I feel that I have to operate the same way when it comes to my students. I give out first- and second-degree ranks in the hopes that the student will someday fully embody what the rank title implies. I do that because I care about people.*

ground in the martial arts, I feel that it is a courtesy of mine to acknowledge their previous martial arts experience. Some may feel that if they fight against someone holding a Bujinkan dojo second-degree black belt rank, they will win because they have a long history of experience in the martial arts. I watch them move. I give out a rank as an encouragement, because they seem to have a certain feeling for the technique, and hope that someday they will be truly skilled.

SKH: I understand that that approach is very Japanese. *Sakizuke*, that procedure is referred to, right? Over here in Japan, if you give a man a rank higher than what he deserves, he will quietly go off and train in private until he is capable of living up to the license he holds. I suppose it is a very good way of motivating your Japanese students.

In the Western world, it is totally different. If you as the grandmaster of ninjutsu gave a man a degree as a means of challenging him to improve, he will mistake that honorary degree for the real thing and go off to set up his own ninjutsu academy under *your* name. It has happened so many times in America and Europe already.

MH: I do not have any intention of wheeling and dealing or operating cleverly. I have nothing to gain or lose by giving out these ranks. That's just the way I walk my path. I will be happy if only one or two persons out of all the thousands of students become real. That is my wish.

RH: You don't mind if someone takes that rank and returns to his homeland to set up a school, and then is seen by others as being obviously unqualified to teach ninjutsu? It doesn't bother you that the name and reputation of your dojo and tradition will be degraded?

MH: It just doesn't matter to me. That's why it's great that we have this opportunity to bring this book out and let the public know the meaning behind our dan ranks. I think the time has come to let the facts be known. If the time were not right, I would not need to make any comment.

RH: Are you really telling us that you don't care whether your dan grades have any value or not?

MH: It is not a matter of whether the degree ranks have value or not. Any perceived value is totally subjective anyway. Value is in the mind of the beholder. What is important here is to know the facts of just how the degree licenses are given out. It is also true that the time has come for certain people to feel embarrassed if they are satisfied with certificates of rank that were based solely on the premature hopes that those persons would someday develop skills worthy of the title they carry. Many highly-skilled Bujinkan dojo instructors are now moving out into the world. A person may claim that he has such-and-such a rank, but I can say that even though the rank is issued under my authority, it cannot be right. After that, it is up to the individual. It is up to his own effort to succeed or fail.

I do not even think about such things as the Bujinkan dojo reputation being disgraced because of my actions. The whole world is our training hall, so of course when certain students stumble or fail the whole world will see the Bujinkan tempering process in operation. If critics want to call that a disgrace, there is nothing that I can do about it. Really, the time has come to state that publicly. If we state all this in our book, people will have to understand.

It was all a matter of waiting for the right time. We had to go through the years of growth before moving out into the public. If each of our instructors is strong enough now, that is all that counts. That's what is important. Each instructor will have to stand or fall based on his own name. His dojo will carry his name, not mine. His success or failure is his own, not mine. I think it's an appropriate time for all you senior instructors to be on your own now.

SKH: That's a big step. I don't know whether I am really ready yet to be out there on my own or not.

MH: You already are, Hayes-san. You already are.

I was brought up by my alcoholic father, so things like that, bold survival tactics, became a natural part of my personality. A feel for actual fighting was there in me already.

Hensojutsu, the ninja's method of assuming the mind and character of someone else, in order to attain the quality of invisibility in the eyes of enemies. Ultimately, the ninja's technique of blending into current surroundings and events is based on his ability to cultivate a free, adaptive, and happily pure heart.

The application of the technique called *hisaku,* in which a neck attack is coupled with a body-crushing scissors choke. The two chokes applied together symbolize the power of the martial heart in chaining the warrior's intentions from one to the other in seamless progression.

Shinken dori. Masaaki Hatsumi uses a small concealed *tetsubo* iron bar to gain control of his attacker's sword while applying a simultaneous *shakoken* palm-claw strike to the face.

Fundo karame tori is a technique in which the chain is used to ensnare the adversary's sword blade.

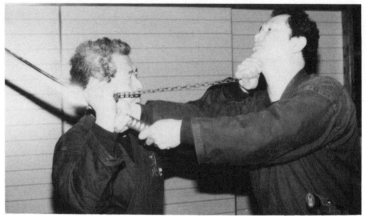

In the eye- and mind-clouding method known as *sanzu no metsubushi*, the *kage no nito* "double-shadow sword" prevents the invasion of evil.

As soon as the swordsman resists, one weight of the chain is shifted and freed to sail into the adversary's chin, while the other weight is smashed into his sword-gripping right hand.

Shuriken goho uchi throwing blade technique is an opportunity to apply the ninja's *bunshin* illusion of being several different characters at the same time. The illusion of several competing bodies is also a symbol of the illusion of having several conflicting motives, or a "divided heart," when in truth the ninja's strong intentions are totally unified.

The chain links of the *kusari kogama* bind and restrict evil, and the sickle then cuts away the harmful influence now ensnared. The *manji shuriken* star blade guides the ninja to spiritual enlightenment.

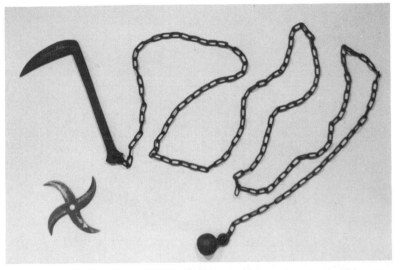

Symbolizing the burning through of worldly desires, the flaming *kaen kusarigama* flies through blackness to bring light to the ninja's heart.

A young Masaaki Hatsumi trains in the *jutte jutsu* iron truncheon art with his teacher To-shitsugu Takamatsu thirty years ago.

The *jutte* catches and jams the swordsman's weapon, [as an older Hatsumi carries the teaching to the future].

As the defender employs the *jutte* over the years, his skills evolve to the point of causing the adversary's downfall by means of his own weapon.

M*arishiten no kamae*, the posture of the guardian divinity Marishi.

When I first met Takamatsu-sensei . . . he admonished me to train, holding in mind that I am a mere insect. "Even an insect," he told me, "if it holds on to a horse's tail, can go for thousands of miles. Therefore, you hold on, too."

When the wind blows, the staff will twirl. The body is light, the body flows. It is not the ninja's power, but the spirit of his *bojutsu* art.

Seigan no kamae, "True eye" staff-fighting posture.

Goku no kamae fighting attitude.

Tensei no kamae, "Heaven's voice" posture.

Mumyo no kamae, "No light" staff-fighting attitude.

Tate no kamae shielding posture.

Tomeya no kamae arrow interception posture.

Yoki no kamae, "Eerie spirit projection," crushes boulders, creates the wind, and summons the storm. *Yojutsu* "arts of weird airs" and *genjutsu* "arts of illusion" cause perceptions to change in the air like a mirage.

With *ganko issen*, a sudden glint of light from the eyes is directed at the attacker to down him. This is the basis for the ninja's *kanashibari* "spirit immobilization" and *toate* "striking down from a distance" techniques.

*M*uto dori unarmed defense against the blade. As the attacker cuts down with a live blade, you use subtle flowing body movement to slip in and catch the deadly weapon just as you would grab a darting bee out of the air.

Jumonji no kamae is the bodily symbol of those warriors whose hearts respect peace, those who realize a sense of justice and extend hands of peace to the spirit of universal nature. Evil ones, however, cannot even come close to the essence of justice. The cross embodied by the *jumonji* postural attitude has an especially powerful meaning in the spiritual lore of the Western world. Just like the devil himself who is thrown into a state of fierce anguish and frustration upon viewing the cross as a symbol of the truly sacred, just as no enemy of holiness can bear to dwell in the presence of the cross, this is the posture that forces concealed evil to show its true face.

Gokui secrets are transmitted only through the vibrations of sound. The timeless knowledge cannot take the form of written words, nor the form of drawn illustrations, nor the form of moving pictures. Only through sound can these truths be handed on. The heartbeat will awaken the dream lying dormant in the recesses of the mind. This is the essence of *bufu*, the martial tradition.

Masaaki Hatsumi
Toratsugu

2
ORIGINS AND LANGUAGE

In the autumn of 1986, my own personal path of warrior exploration had taken me well past my teacher's Japan to the once-inaccessible mainland of China. Stepping into the footprints of Toshitsugu Takamatsu more than sixty years after this teacher of my teacher had made his journeys through *Chungkuo*, the Central Kingdom, I set out to find any remaining hints of the vast and legendary Chinese warrior past against which Toshitsugu Takamatsu, the Mongolian Tiger, had set himself in the rough and tumble days of China in the 1920s.

Rumiko and our daughters far away and safely at home, I had awakened at dawn to see the mists rise from the surface of the Pearl River as it drifted timelessly through old Canton. Up and across the ancient sleepy land mass of China, I made my way northward to Chengdu, homeland of Chinese bamboo forests, wild pandas, and screaming golden monkeys. As each mile passed, it became increasingly heartbreaking to realize that few of the original martial art training halls and temples had made it through the hysterically violent and self-destructive insanity of what the Chinese called their Cultural Revolution. So very little of what I had seen was left over from the days of the young wanderer Takamatsu.

From Han China, I had made my way up and onto the Tibetan Plateau. From a base in Lhasa, I explored the monastic holds of Sera and Drepung, former strongholds of the Tibetan monastic tradition. Once virtual cities of holy men with resident populations numbering in the thousands, the monastic fortresses are now mere ghosts of their former selves with only dozens of monks where once lived thousands.

This had been my second trip to the rooftop of the world. I had travelled to the Himalayas the year before as well. Ninjutsu grandmaster Masaaki Hatsumi had suggested that the roots of Japan's ancient ninja legacy stretched far past China and on out along the legendary Silk Road trading route. Again this year I had arranged to venture into the awesome stretches of the Himalayas of Tibet in search of that which has fascinated me since my own preschool days.

I continued across Tibet, visiting what was left of the bastions of the once-powerful Tibetan monastic tradition. My questions about the battling *dop-dop* fighter monks of pre-communist Tibet brought little more response than wistful smiles from most of the few remaining Tibetan monks. The two aged veterans I was able to locate were hesitant to discuss their past. Many of the brotherhood had been gunned down by the invading Chinese three decades ago for knowing too much about physical protection of their homeland and loved ones. Perhaps it was the novelty of at last being approached by someone interested in the legacy of the Tibetan monk combatants, perhaps it was more due to spite for the occupying Chinese who are struggling to appear so humane and civilized in a search for profitable trade after so many years of brutality, but at last the two finally acquiesced. In the dim light of yak butter lamps and incense clouds, I was given the requested insights into the combat tactics of the fearsome *dop-dop* fighter monks.

From Tibet I went on to Nepal, and then continued on to India. In India, I had made my way up to mountaintop Dharamsala, government in exile center of Tenzin Gyatso, the fourteenth Dalai Lama of Tibet. While there, I was able to meet with representatives of the Tibetan exile population. My interviews had ranged from militant members of what remains of Tibet's underground resistance forces, to the director of the Tibetan Medical Institute, to a personal interview with His Holiness the Dalai Lama himself.

Once referred to as the god–king of six million Tibetans, the

Dalai Lama is indeed a commanding figure in person. Having been forced to flee his own native land almost three decades ago after Chinese troops shelled his summer residence following the Tibetan people's abortive attempt at protesting the brutally oppressive Chinese occupation, Tenzin Gyatso has maintained his residence in northwestern India. He must at the same time live the life of a devout Buddhist monk seeking to aid the spiritual enlightenment of the world, while also working as an able political figure in the cause of attaining national freedom for his now enslaved mountain kingdom.

Hatsumi-sensei is in the kitchen of his *bettaku*, preparing more hot water for our tea. I pull a dark-brown paper bag from beneath my notebooks and place it on the table in front of me. The bag is imprinted with Indian and English characters across its front, and contains my *omiage* ("greeting presents") for my teacher. These presents, given whenever returning from a trip or, in smaller scale, whenever visiting someone's home in Japan, are a crucial social lubricant not to be overlooked in importance when working at maintaining a relationship.

Characteristically, my eccentric teacher seems to place very little importance on this present-giving ritual. As I have discovered over years of being around my teacher, he seems almost proud of his contrary nature that enjoys foregoing things sacrosanct to most Japanese in favor of a more international mindset and behavioral style. This refusal to be classified as a Japanese, preferring to be seen as having no country and no limits to his freedom, once prompted the grandmaster to label himself a UFO.

A seeming indifference to receiving customary gifts notwithstanding, I nevertheless always keep my eyes open for suitable presents for this man for whom it seems so difficult to choose gifts. What do you give the man whose home is already overflowing with decorator curios, artworks, books, and what is probably the world's most extensive private collection of historical Japanese weapons, manuscripts, and scrolls?

Hatsumi-sensei returns to the room with a fresh kettle of hot water for tea. I use the momentary interruption to slide the dark-brown paper bag across the table and announce that it contains a few small gifts from my trip through the Himalayas. Curious, the grandmaster peeks inside. Interestingly, instead of lifting the bag for a better view, he lowers his head to allow his sight to penetrate its opening.

I pick up the bag and pull out a huge iron Tibetan doorlock key on a long thick leather strap. I explain to Dr. Hatsumi that it is a key to one of the old locks of Sera monastery, and was used as one of the standard fighting tools of Tibet's *dop-dop* warrior monks. Along the lines of the ninja's *kusarifundo* (weighted-chain weapon) as used in the Bujinkan dojo training method, the heavy key could be whirled and slung out at targets and then quickly withdrawn. Seemingly pleased with the unusual gift, he jots a few details about the key weapon in his notebook and looks up again.

From the brown bag, I withdraw a folded white silk scarf and drape it over my teacher's neck in the Tibetan tradition of greeting a special person. The scarf itself is strictly a symbolic adornment. Lightly dusted with powder and so finely woven as to be almost transparent, the Tibetan *khata* could never be worn as a garment for holding in warmth. I explain the Tibetan scarf custom to Masaaki Hatsumi, and further explain that this particular scarf is a special present for him, having been blessed by His Holiness the Dalai Lama himself.

I am pleasantly surprised at just how pleased my teacher seems to be at receiving the scarf. He gets his camera and has Rumiko take several snapshots of me placing the *khata* over his shoulders. He comments that he considers this scarf as some sort of superb omen as to very positive things to come in the future. Folding the scarf and placing it on the table beside him, the grandmaster reaches out and turns on the tape recorder.

MH: What a remarkable person you are, Hayes-san. You were able to publish your novel *Tulku,* all about the invasion of Tibet and the escape of the Dalai Lama, and then on top of that, you were actually able to get an audience with the real Dalai Lama himself. Your fiction was your bridge to real world accomplishment. I feel very honored to be given this gift scarf from the Dalai Lama, just because I am your teacher. I feel very grateful. I would like to send him a letter of thanks and a painting of mine as a present for his kindness to you.

SKH: Years ago, you told me one time that the roots of the Japanese ninja tradition stretched far beyond China to the Silk Road and the Himalayas. Wherever the Buddhist tradition went, you told me, the warrior arts flourished as a means of protecting the enlightenment teachings from eradication by the enemies of the faith. You also mentioned that you would like to speak with the Tibetan lamas. Do you remember that conversation we had?

Anything that must have a specific shape or form can easily be ruined forever. That's why I want my art to be formless.

Well, you are the *soke*, and sometimes the grandmaster has to rely on his students to fulfill things that his duties might prevent him from doing. So I went off to try to meet the Dalai Lama of Tibet as suggested by you. I also considered it a test of my own powers of resourcefulness. What a challenge, huh, an interview with the god-king of Tibet? I like to believe that our art relates to power at all levels, not just physical combat techniques. Power, in all its manifestations, is a fascinating topic of study.

MH: I am told that somebody wrote an article in an American martial arts magazine claiming that I do not have much power in my technique. Of course, that individual does not know me at all. But that's okay. It's to be expected. Only the ones who really know what this art is will be able to appreciate it. I think that's the way a man should live. Those who do not understand the essence behind why we teach the way we do will get themselves killed. This is very important. This is the sense that you must have. Do not get attached to the idea of going through life elegantly and proudly. Walk simply. Walk honestly and directly. Don't strut through life like a *yakuza* street punk.

For that reason, Takamatsu-sensei told me that the goal is to become a *tatsujin* (complete human being), a total being. What I want to say here is, if you look like a martial artist, that's the end for you. Especially nowadays with guns so commonplace. If you look like you are a real threat to someone, he will just pull out a gun and blow you away. It's so easy to take the life of anyone, even one who struts around boasting about his so-called high rank in the martial arts. Having thoughts on fighting all the time, having animal-like thoughts all the time, if those are the only thoughts a person has, he will end up dead before his time. He will be destroyed easily.

SKH: It's very difficult getting that across in America. If you don't strut around and play the role of the tough guy, the public just goes blind to any real martial skills you might have to teach. I see it as a real weakness, a dangerous weakness. If the goal is self-protection, the worst thing to do is goad on the world by boasting to everybody about how much tougher than them you are.

MH: Getting caught up in a set way of having to move, do things, or respond should be seen as a danger to a martial artist. Very valuable Japanese cultural treasures, take the Kinkakuji Golden Pavilion for example, are extremely vulnerable because of their specific form and expected appearance. If the Kinkakuji is severely damaged or burns to the ground, that is the end of that treasure. People could not accept a modified or altered or new Kinkakuji. Because everyone knows what to expect, if the landmark is altered even slightly, the tourists would know that something is wrong. Anything that must have a specific shape or form can easily be ruined forever. That's why I want my art to be formless.

SKH: I agree wholeheartedly. But it is hard getting that across. It shouldn't be hard; it's common sense. But it is hard getting that across to so many martial artists in America.

MH: The problem starts when you think that you can convince everybody. Each individual is different. He has his own way of thinking. Just like there is day and night, human beings are divided into basic types. One type may work better by day, others may work better by night. Some have high blood-pressure problems and some have low blood-pressure problems; in between there is the normal one.

RH: A lot of our fundamental techniques have names in the taijutsu book. Some names are very difficult to figure out. How were they named?

MH: In the old days?

RH: Yes.

MH: Japanese written characters are unique, and each character has its own meaning. For example, there is a technique we call *Koyoku.* The *ko* portion translates as "eagle's talon." *Yoku* means "wing." The name *Koyoku* could be translated as "talon and wing." It is possible that the movement may look like the feeling presented in the written characters making up the name.

Hicho is literally translated as "flying bird," as I mentioned the other day. But in its martial art application, perhaps this is not always the most appropriate way to think of it. Ostriches do not fly. There is a more subtle way to interpret it. When people hear a reference to *hicho no kamae* posture or *hicho* technique, they

will imagine a technique that has something to do with leaping or flying. Doesn't that make sense to you? When you write it down, it reads "flying bird." But the technique itself is not really like that, is it?

SKH: I've often wondered about that myself; why does the technique called "flying bird" involve no leaping or leaving the ground?

MH: There are so many different kinds of birds, birds that swim, birds that walk around, and birds that fly. You have to take these three very different kinds of birds into consideration. Birds are supposed to be night blind. They cannot see at night. But an owl can. Since an owl is different from the other kinds of birds, it receives a bad description. "Night owls" are generally thought to be odd or different people, right?

RH: So you mean techniques were named as they were because their movements are reflected in the name, but each name also had so many shadings?

MH: Yes, yes. But what is in the technique is much more important than the history of the name. Do not get trapped by the literal names that are written in the *densho* (historically transmitted) scrolls.

RH: There are so many difficult words used as the technique names.

MH: Yes, that's true. The reason why they used such difficult words was that in the old days, they had to keep it secret, just in case the scroll might be stolen. Or they purposely used misleading words. They might even use the completely opposite word. They might identify a method of attacking an adversary as a defensive technique, for example. The way of pronouncing the written words may be the same, but different characters might be used. So if someone looks at one of the scrolls, he will not be able to learn anything of value if he does not have a good teacher to initiate him. It will lead him to developing techniques for how to lose instead of how to win! So learning it from a good teacher is the only way to know that you are learning it the right way.

Well, this is one of the methods behind the way they wrote the old *densho*. Therefore, it is so important to realize that you have to learn this art from a properly trained instructor.

SKH: Finding the right instructor is so difficult for new students these days. There are so many phonies, so many imitation ninja masters out there. Even the Bujinkan label is not a guarantee of high-level training any more, now that unqualified people use your name so freely in setting themselves up as masters.

MH: Some people attempt to study this art for a couple of years. They interpret the techniques all wrong, and then they publish these incorrect assumptions in the magazines or books, and it only ends up confusing the sincere people. Only those who can answer these kinds of questions like I do are the ones who are qualified to write about these things. So this will be an important point for anybody who wants to write about this art, or pick out good books about this art for their reading.

SKH: Uh-oh! I could fall under that negative category with my books. I would hate to think that I had mislead anyone.

MH: Of course not. Of course not. I am not talking about your books when I refer to unqualified people speaking as authorities. Because I chose you to write this book with me, the public will know that you are the one qualified to write about our art in English.

SKH: All kinds of rumors are flying around, now that the art of ninjutsu has become so in demand. I had even heard that some people over here in Japan thought that you did not want me writing books about this art.

MH: People say that I change from moment to moment, that I am so hard to figure out. But when they actually sit down and talk with me, they will realize that the baffling way that I talk and act is a part of what it means to be a real martial artist. Being too predictable is a dangerous way to live if you are a warrior.

RH: But Japanese instructors live here and see you often, they hear you talk all the time, they may have some questions they want to ask, they may have some doubts also. They can find an answer to those doubts or those questions in a single word you say at the training hall before they even have the chance to pose the question. So I would assume that less misunderstanding occurs around here?

MH: No, it happens here all the time, too. You know very well the stories of those students who misunderstood and angrily walked out even after decades of my giving them knowledge. So I think it is not a matter of distance. It is not a matter of whether you are always in the training hall. It is something that is up to the student's heart and motivations.

Tsuki kage no	("The village
terasuno sato wa	once shined down upon by the moon
nakeredomo	is gone.
nagamuru hito no	Looking up at the moon again,
kokoro ni zo sumu.	the village lives on in his heart.")

This was written by Honen (1133-1212), who left the practice of the Tendai sect of Buddhism to found the Jodo sect. He was the teacher of Shinran, the founder of the Jodo Shin Shu Buddhist sect. I like the feeling of that poem. I can identify with that sentiment. I would like to live on in the hearts of those few people who admire me, just as that village lives on in the heart of that displaced person in the poem. I would be really happy with that alone.

RH: We are so pleased to have this chance to speak with you one-on-one today. We can listen to you and hear so many interesting stories from you. In the past, so many times, we had to admit that we could not understand your actions.

MH: I am sure that is true. If you have any moments of doubt or lack of understanding in anything, just write to me without hesitation. I would like to say this to all the people of the world, but I can only handle Japanese. As you know, when language is translated, sometimes certain feelings cannot be expressed as well as in the original language. So that may be a difficulty. But as you grow to know me better, as you spend more time with me, language barriers gradually disappear. Sometimes my taijutsu movements translate better than an interpreter. I have never really studied any English, so it is kind of strange isn't it, that you so well understand my heart? But then, I talk with my body. I talk with my heart.

RH: Your language is the language of the heart.

MH: I think that is important.

RH: We know an American university professor who studies Tendai *mikkyo* in Japan with a quite high-ranking Tendai priest. Our friend's monk name Jikai incorporates the "Ji" part of his teacher's name. Is that the way it is done here in the Bujinkan dojo, too? All the master instructors seem to have *ryu* ("dragon") in their names, just like the *ryu* in your Byakuryuoh name.

MH: That's right, it is the same. Hayes-san, let me take this opportunity here to give you the warrior name *Kinryu* ("Gold Dragon"). It is appropriate for you to have that name after passing the test of avoiding my sword from behind that time. Also, you were the first non-Japanese person to receive my gold dragon award medallion as well. Your lucky number won you my gold dragon painting at the *Daikomyosai* [Masaaki Hatsumi's annual formal birthday celebration banquet] the night before you passed the *godan* test. From now on, you should use the name Kinryu.

RH: Ninja were referred to by different names. There is the word *shinobi*. Historically, when did this word come into use to describe ninja?

MH: Otomo Sainyu once said that they used different kanji-written characters.

RH: What did they write? What were the kanji?

MH: At the time of Shotoku Taishi, in the late sixth century, the words were written differently but still pronounced "shinobi." *Shi no bi* was written that long time ago with the kanji characters that mean "secrets of will (intention)," or "to employ the ability of will (intention)." That is one theory of how this old style *shinobi* was used to describe the original historical ninja.

Another theory is that there were words like *shinobikomu* ("to sneak in") or *shinobigaeshi* ("to conceal oneself atop a roof or wall and from there gather information or attack the enemy from above"). Since the people who were later called ninja were skilled at these methods, it later developed that this *shinobi* from these words came to mean the persons we describe as ninja today.

In the beginning, the names of many of the ninjutsu traditions and lineages came from the names of the regions in which they operated. Ninja from the Iga area were called *Iga no ninja* or *Iga no mono*. Also, it must be remembered that the names used within the actual ninja groups themselves had to be held onto as highly protected secrets, so they were not always known by outsiders. Outsiders rarely ever knew the family names of the ninja, so they simply refered to them as "ninja from Iga," or "ninja from Koga," and so forth. Sometimes the regions from which they operated were much more familiar to everyone than the family names themselves. This is still very much the practice for Japanese people living in the country. People are identified by the areas in which they live rather than by name. So I would assume that is how the name started. There is no definitely established theory on when this word *shinobi* first came into use. There are so many theories.

RH: This is a question that we are asked often by students. They say they hear a lot about Togakure ryu, but they do not hear much about Kumogakure ryu, or the other ryu in our history. Is there anything you can say about the other ryu?

MH: There is a theory that the fundamental base for the ninja fighting method is *Gyokko ryu koshijutsu*, which was adapted in Japan from an older original Chinese fighting system. It is my feeling that this Gyokko ryu method was not simply transplanted whole to Japan. It was absorbed and adapted to relate with the indigenous Japanese fighting methods of the period. Then this *koshijutsu* (muscle-and-organ tearing system) was later expanded upon, and evolved into the Japanese *koppojutsu* (bone-breaking method). According to Takamatsu, ninja from Iga and Koga areas mastered *koshijutsu* and *koppojutsu* as a part of their combat training. As you know, if you cannot properly do *taijutsu*, there is no way you can do sword or spear techniques either.

RH: Do you ever label the techniques for the students, so that they know which historical tradition produced which method?

MH: The reason why we do not pay a lot of attention to the specifics of each ryu is that we are studying all nine systems in a manner that produces one set of internalized skills in our student. Of course, each of the historical ryu did have its own characteristic points. For example, the Togakure ryu of ninjutsu handed

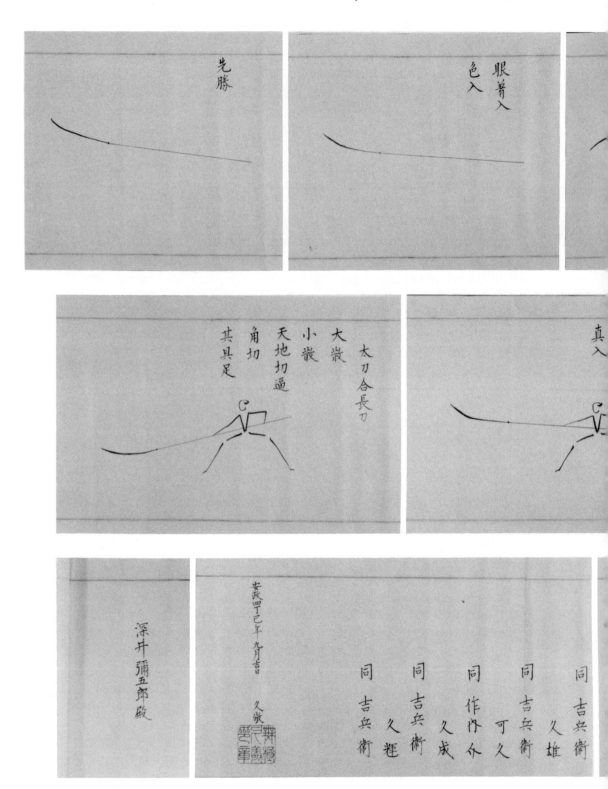

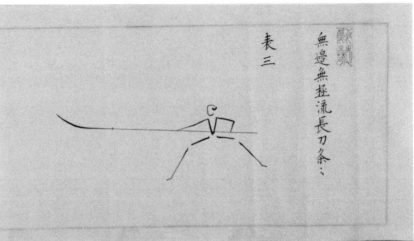

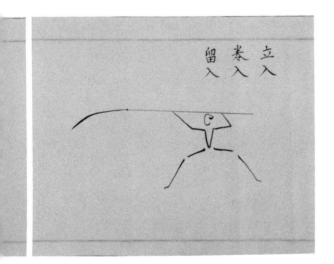

Battlefield long-weapon techniques from the scroll of *Muhen mukyoku ryu*, written about 130 years ago, and now in the private collection of Masaaki Hatsumi. [Turn to the end of Chapter 5 for demonstrations of the *bisento*.]

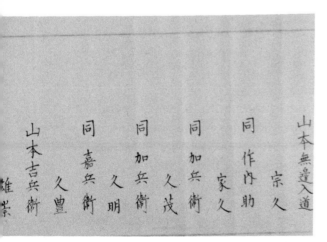

Each person is differently structured. Therefore, each will create a method of movement that best suits him. I am in search of the kind of students who can reach the same level I have, but as unique artists in their own right.

down its *ninpo taijutsu*, along with some secretly developed tools and weapons, such as *senban* (four-pointed throwing blades), *shinodake* (thin bamboo underwater-breathing tube), and *shuko* (climbing claws). These were distinctive weapons exclusive to the Togakure ryu.

What is distinctive about the Kumogakure ryu is a similar form of *taijutsu*, along with *kamayari* (sickle spears). That was their secret weapon. They also had a special cedar tree climbing method known as *ippon sugi nobori* for going up those straight cedar trunks. That special climbing tool was also used as a weapon, along the order of our weighted-chain flail.

RH: So the principles of the combat training in each ryu overlapped somewhat?

MH: It might help if I explain this all in simple terms. Basically, the ninja's hand-to-hand fighting method was taijutsu, sometimes referred to as *koshijutsu*, sometimes *dakentaijutsu*, or *yawara*, or even *jujutsu*. The terms changed and varied as the years went on. Sometimes it was called *koshijutsu* or *koppojutsu* or only *te* [literally translated as "hand", implying "hand-to-hand"]. So the basic core was taijutsu, and after they had mastered taijutsu they learned to employ the special weapons of their style or system.

In the taijutsu training of each specific tradition, there may be slight differences in body postures, or the names given to specific fists, but if I were to classify it technique by technique now and try to teach it that way, it would be an enormous task. Therefore, right now, the Togakure ryu (originally established at the beginning of the Kamakura period in 1185) is representative of the entire collection of nine ryu. Even though we refer to our training system as being based on Togakure ryu combat techniques, we may in fact be using a method from Kumogakure ryu. If there is a strong enough demand to classify these methods individually, I could do it in the future. But the basic principles and methods are the same.

SKH: I suppose it is a matter of whether a person is studying this art as an intellectual historian, or as a practitioner who intends to put the teachings to work in his life. Sometimes, I think some of the students can get too caught up in the technical details and lose the essence of the feeling behind the technique. To me, the results are what counts, not the mere technique itself.

MH: In the old days, they used to use a flint-and-steel striker to light a fire, but today we can use a [butane] lighter. It is the same with the history of what you are studying and teaching as your martial art. Don't make it more complicated than it needs to be.

At the same time, it should be remembered that you, for example, Hayes-san are built differently than Oguri-san or me. Each person is differently structured. Therefore, each will create a method of movement that best suits him. I was given the title of *soke*, and just like there is one Picasso in the world, there is only one Masaaki Hatsumi. After Picasso died, there was no Picasso. Though there is only one Picasso, there are others like Chagall, Gaugain, and so forth. So I am in search of the kind of students who can reach the same level I have, but as unique artists in their own right.

This is the way I feel. It is not necessary for you [or anyone] to be too concerned with cataloguing this technique or that. It is sufficient to think of all our training as the Bujinkan dojo method. Since the basic principles are all the same, the fundamentals are the same. The grip of the sword might be slightly different, certain techniques might be slightly different, names of techniques may be different, but sometimes even though the names are different, the movements themselves are similar. I hope this will be a satisfactory answer. I would like to add that after this it is up to the individual student to gain more knowledge.

RH: We are asked by people whether you possess any scrolls from our nine lineages, and whether you would be willing to show those scrolls to anyone who wanted to see them.

MH: Sure. Of course. I can show them the scrolls.

SKH: One well-known American martial arts book writer would only refer to you as a "ninjutsu historian." He even got your name slightly wrong in his ninjutsu book. A nice sarcastic touch, I thought. Anyway, he indicated to me once in a private

If the scrolls are stolen, or something happens to the scrolls, they will not make any sense to those persons who have not been initiated. It's like giving money to a cat; the cat has no way of appreciating or using it.

conversation at the Budokan that unless he could see the actual Togakure ryu scrolls, he could not believe that our ryu was an authentic historical entity.

MH: (Pleasantly.) Oh? Really? He did?

SKH: He wrote a little book on ninjutsu, which was actually a collection of some of the Japanese children's ninja legends and a rough translation of the espionage chapter from the Sun Tsu Chinese war treatise. It wasn't what I have come to know as authentic ninjutsu. Anyway, his book has been read by many people, and that is why they may have come up with these questions about the scrolls. They all want to know about the scrolls. Is there a scroll relating to each of the nine ryu?

MH: Yes, I have them. I even have many *makimono* scrolls from martial arts ryu with which we are not associated at all. But what you have to consider as most important here is that a *makimono* could in a way be compared with a bank check. There is a signature and an amount written there, but how much is that check really worth? How much is in the bank to back up that check you have in your hand? Even though you may have those scrolls, if you don't have enough training and knowledge to interpret the scrolls, you don't have much money in your account, your checks will not be worth much. What I mean is that unless the person who looks at the scrolls is really trained in the art, he will have no idea of the scroll's value.

That is the essence of the Japanese martial arts *makimono* scroll. What is written in a *makimono* are certain key points only. Those key points, those cryptic highlights, those few carefully chosen words expand in meaning to the reader who knows what he is looking for. Even if the scrolls are stolen, or something happens to the scrolls, they will not make any sense to those persons who have not been initiated. It's like giving money to a cat; the cat has no way of appreciating or using it.

There is a theory that ninja were farmers, but it would not be correct to mistakenly imagine them as peasants. Also there is the theory that ninja were merchants. So there is no one single established theory as to just exactly where the ninja phenomena came from.

At the same time, as you know because you have been teaching this art for many years, some martial arts' scrolls were destroyed during the war, or some were burned in housefires. Because of cases like that, some scrolls had to be rewritten. The person who had to rewrite them had to rely on his memory alone, and he put down the things that he thought were important.

SKH: A martial art's scroll of authority, handed from one master to the next, is more in the form of an icon, then.

MH: Scrolls are considered to be sacred, and I agree. Just like an American flag is considered to be sacred, even though it is just a symbol, I think the true *makimono* is a sacred object. Therefore, luckily I was given all those scrolls by Takamatsu-sensei, and if anybody asks me to show them, I will be happy to do that at any time.

I also have a lot of other historical martial arts scrolls in my collection as well, such as the scrolls of the Kimura ryu and Shin Kage ryu. Occasionally, old scrolls are sold through antique dealers or bookstores that specialize in that kind of old manuscripts. But I can well see what the scroll wants to say. The smell of the ink, the shape and quality of the calligraphy reveal the writer's personality and level of advancement in skill as a martial artist. I can see all that through their writing and even the quality of paper they used. Surely, the scrolls are important things.

SKH: Where do you get all these scrolls?

MH: I have many, many scrolls in my personal collection. Besides the scrolls given to me by Takamatsu-sensei, I have also made quite a collection of those scrolls from other martial lineages. I am in touch with a lot of antique dealers and bookshops, and purchase scrolls from all over Japan. Just feeling and looking at the scrolls, I can sense what kind of techniques the art embodied, what kind of skills were possessed by the writer. I look at the scrolls that way. Does this help? Is this what you wanted to hear?

RH: When ninjutsu was coming into being, there was strong influence from religion and spiritual practices. I heard that *shugendo* had an influence on the development of ninjutsu. What is your opinion on this?

MH: As you know, our Kukishin ryu developed in the Kumano area. There, the *Amatsu Tatarahibun* document is still preserved to this day. I read through and interpreted the entire volume. Also I was given all related materials along that line by Takamatsu-sensei. The old-time shugenja walked about the mountains with their *shakujo* ringed staff and trained in their martial arts. This is one theory.

Religious missionaries had to be strong to help people. Daruma Taishi [Indian spiritual teacher Bodhidharma, said to have introduced the practice of martially related physical exercises and zen meditation principles to Chinese monks in the early sixth century] was also that way, too. He was said to be good at *bojutsu*. Combat tools were a part of what was imported along with meditation and visualization methods.

There are different kinds of religion, depending on which part of the country you explore. On Tendai sect's Hie Mountain, there were *sohei* (monk soldiers), and on Kuki Mountain, there were Kuki shugenja. I would say that if there was any direct influence on the art of ninjutsu, it was from the Kuki shugenja. There could have been an influence from the Dewa Sanzan, the three holy mountain peaks of Yamagata Prefecture, in which the Haguro shugenja trained. On Hie Mountain, there was Buddhist influence from the monk soldiers, as I mentioned.

There were some samurai who became farmers after losing in battle, so they were not just simple plain farmers. In the old times, *bushi* warriors were usually engaged in farming, and when there was an emergency, they were called into action as samurai once again.

Wasn't that the same in Viet Nam, too? Those people were farmers by profession, but became soldiers out of necessity. There is a theory that ninja were farmers, but it would not be correct to mistakenly imagine them as peasants. Also there is the theory that ninja were merchants.

Omi shonin, the merchants of Omi, now Shiga Prefecture, are a good example. They disguised themselves as merchants. They travelled all over the country selling their merchandise, but that was just a cover story. In actuality, they were gathering information. So there is no one single established theory as to just exactly where the ninja phenomena came from.

RH: So these religious and spiritual traditions were a part of all that lead up to the development of ninjutsu as its own independent warrior art.

MH: Think of the ninja as our foundation. Don't try to put the shugenja ahead of the ninja historically. You will not be mistaken if you think that there were the ninja, and then the shugenja appeared in the story. In the same way, there were the ninja, and then the Buddhist influence became strong in Japan. So *mikkyo* is considered to be an influence that arrived after the original ninjutsu concept was formed; the ninja did not emerge from *mikkyo* as their establishing source. If you put ninjutsu behind *mikkyo* in the timeline of history, then you will be speaking from the monk's point of view of the story. Is this understandable?

RH: Just because there was the practice of shugendo going on at the same general time and area, it doesn't mean that shugendo was the source for ninjutsu. There were, however, some elements of shugendo in the ninja's arts.

MH: Yes, yes. That's right. That's a good way to look at it.

From the *ichimonji no kamae* posture, Masaaki Hatsumi receives Stephen Hayes's lunging punch attack.

Cutting the punch short by attacking the attack, defender Hatsumi stops his adversary's momentum.

Before the second attacking punch can be thrown, he slams a right lifting kick into attacker's jaw.

A grab-and-punch attack setup.

Masaaki Hatsumi defends by slipping in and past the advancing punch, applying a left lifting elbow strike to the attacking arm as he avoids the punch.

When attacker Hayes responds with a left follow-up punch, defender Hatsumi counters with a right punch into the wrist of the attacking left hand.

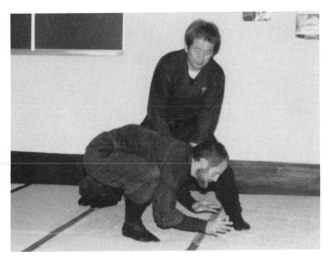

The defender then quickly slides his right foot out and to the side, knocking out the attacker's support leg to take him to the ground.

A natural standing position.

Masaaki Hatsumi responds to a kicking attack by angling his body to cause the attack to miss its target, while sending out a groin kick of his own.

Without retracting his foot, defender Hatsumi swats inward with the same kicking foot to unbalance the stunned attacker.

Maintaining the *hicho no kamae* ("flying bird" fighting posture), Masaaki Hatsumi observes his student Stephen Hayes as he approaches from the *ichimonji no kamae* posture.

Dr. Hatsumi suddenly drops his left foot while attacking his adversary's leading hand with a strike from the back of his left hand.

He immediately bounces his strike up from its target and continues with a left fingertip spear to his victim's eyes.

With a counterclockwise body twist, Masaaki Hatsumi works Stephen Hayes's left arm into an arm bar.

He applies right knee pressure from behind Hayes's left knee to take him to the ground.

Once on the ground, he is immobilized with a double arm bar restraining hold.

As attacker Hayes tightens his grip, defender Hatsumi drops his hips with a clockwise shoulder twist, trapping Hayes's choking arm as he spins around.

Stephen Hayes applies a rear choke hold on Masaaki Hatsumi.

Dr. Hatsumi drops to the ground, exerting wrenching pressure on the shoulder of the trapped arm.

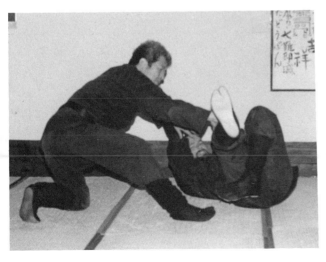

The defender's motion spins attacker Hayes to the ground.

Attacker Stephen Hayes executes a right up-percut punch to the solar plexus.

By allowing his knees to flex and take his torso away from the punch's intended target, Masaaki Hatsumi thwarts the attack passively.

Defender Hatsumi then pivots counterclockwise, and controlling the attacking arm by wedging it in at his own left hip, slings the attacker to the ground.

3
A LIVING ART

Masaaki Hatsumi sits beside his wife Mariko across the little table from Rumiko and me. The tabletop before us has a black steel grilling surface built right into it. Little glasses of water perch on the edge of the table away from the heat of the cooking plate. It is well after the luncheon crowd has come and gone, so finding a table is easy. We are in no particular hurry.

A waitress appears with piles of raw ingredients for our own self-cooked *okonomiyaki* cakes. I like to call these things "Japanese pizza," because of all the tossed-in ingredients, but in truth there is nothing pizza-like about these plate-sized seafood and vegetable pancakes. Liquid batter, shredded cabbage, egg, chopped octopus, finely grated seaweed powder, dried bonito slivers, and a sweet thick brown vegetable and fruit sauce all go in according to preference. We each monitor our own *okonomiyaki* as it cooks before us.

The restaurant owner approaches Dr. Hatsumi with a request. They are celebrating their restaurant's recent expansion. As part of the festivities, they are asking some of their better-known patrons to paint an impromptu piece of artwork on *ema* wooden

Dr. Masaaki Hatsumi and his wife Mariko (left).

squares that will be hung from the branches of an artificial tree
that has been constructed in the middle of the dining area. We
turn and look around at the tree, its branches already heavy with
the paintings and calligraphy displays. Hatsumi-sensei comments
that he will take the block home and bring his completed painting
back tomorrow. The restaurateur hesitates, knowing that the
doctor is an artist and not wanting his customer to feel put upon,
and then comments that it need not be that complete a work of
art. Something simple is fine; this is all just in the spirit of fun.
The grandmaster states again that he will take the wooden plaque
home for completion. The restaurant owner uncomfortably
realizes he can say no more.

   Dr. Hatsumi picks up another one of the little wooden *ema*
plaques and begins to draw on it as his wife converses with
Rumiko. The grandmaster's brush strokes quickly take shape as a
comically sinister ninja character crawling across the wooden
surface. He then flips the plaque over and autographs the piece
with congratulations on my latest black belt degree/license pro-

motion. He hands me the wooden rectangle and comments with a smile that it is a present for my dojo back in Ohio.

As Hatsumi-sensei joins the women's conversation, I pick up one of the blank rectangles and begin a picture of my own. There in the cockpit of a cartoon flying saucer crouches another comic ninja in historical black garb. I offer my work to the man who likes so much to think of himself as a UFO, with the comment that if the grandmaster ever builds his own dojo, he can put this *ema* offering in there. Everyone at the table looks at the little painting on wood and laughs.

In recent years, I have increasingly come to understand and appreciate the whole life integration of Masaaki Hatsumi the artist. His *ninpo taijutsu* combat movement, his brush strokes, even the way he chooses his words in conversation—all reflect an artist's sensitivities. Beginning with the basics of bodily actions, the artist continues to refine and perfect his crusade for the elimination of the crude, ineffective, inaccurate, and inappropriate. Perhaps it could be said that the true goal of the artist is to let go of all aspects that serve as obstacles to his own ability to successfully deliver direct personal self-expression.

To commit myself to the perfection of the art of martial technique is to confront myself, and in so doing, confront all those aspects of myself that I have allowed to get in my way for a lifetime. It is a form of art that demands total honesty. It is a form of art in which the relentless search for areas of personal weakness and vulnerability takes precedence over the indulgence of enjoying areas of strength and accomplishment.

I am exposed totally every time I move with another practitioner. My body condition is exposed, my attitude is exposed, my fears are exposed, my history is exposed, my vulnerabilities are exposed, my perceptions are exposed, and my sense of humor is exposed. I nakedly show all observers how I relate to pressure with my timing, distance, and awareness of the other's movements against me.

The martial art is the art of facing truth at the razor's edge. I cannot lie with my technique, I cannot blur the edges, I cannot cover inabilities with clever diversions. I tell my truth every time I move.

As my art develops and I enter the arena of sharing my techniques and training methods with others, I come to realize that as a public artist, I am even more exposed than I ever was before. I feel this every time I face a new crowd at a seminar, where I know that my challenge is to make all of them feel something uplifting and enlightening through the movement of my body, intellect, and spirit operating as a single three-dimensional unit. I know that this too is a form of art as naked honesty. I know that I have to mean everything I do. I have to have complete faith in my own experience, skills, strengths, insights, timing, cunning, and luck. I know that everyone out there will be comparing his or her skills and strengths to mine, because they are martial artists, too.

I also know that any slips I make, any less-than-effective movements I permit to take place, will anger and embarrass everyone in the crowd watching me, because that is just what they fear most in themselves. I know that they want me to be successful, because I represent what they themselves would like to be. I also know that they would not be there, or that they will not be there the next time, if I am not as much of the artist as I possibly can be. They are each of them artists themselves. They will only be there for me so long as I have something of inspiration to offer them. The art of the teacher is just that brutally honest. The way of the public artist is just that coldly demanding.

MH: What we are discussing today is a very important topic for all martial artists in the world. I went to America, and one of the reasons I went there was to apologize. I went to apologize to the American students for all the false notions that so many oriental martial arts teachers have given them. The martial arts, in the true sense of why the martial arts were developed over a thousand years ago in Japan, have been totally distorted and perverted today. These foreign students don't know any better, of course, because they believe in what the oriental teachers tell them. Everything has been turned into a sport, an overly regimented or complicated abstract form, or into a false system of violent talk that would have no effectiveness at all on the street.

I do not mean to defile the Japanese martial arts with these comments. That is not my purpose. However, I do want people to know the true histories of where their martial arts came from. Judo, karate, aikido—these are all wonderful arts, and obviously they have many desirable aspects that have attracted millions of

students all over the world. I have experienced all of the popular Japanese martial arts myself, but I wanted to find a true fighting art. I was searching for an art unlimited by any rules, and yet molded in the influence of what could be described as the most dreadful and horrifying rules imaginable. There is nothing more dreadful than the rule that says there are no rules. I had to go through many martial arts, but I finally made it to where I am now.

My stand, based on the training that was handed down to my teacher and through him to me, is that *bugei*, the warrior arts, should be acknowledged and recognized more as actual arts. As arts, these martial methods are an embodiment of peaceful intentions. The martial arts are a manifestation of your intentions to live your life as it should be lived as a total human being. That is what flows on as the basis of the authentic historical martial arts.

SKH: I like that kind of talk. For so many years after I had gotten involved with the martial arts, I had actually forgotten my original childhood motivations for getting involved in the first place. I had turned into the same thing that overtakes so many others—I had come to view the martial arts as a "thing" in and of itself. I was practicing martial techniques for the sake of practicing martial techniques. I had lost any sense of pertinent motivation. I mean by that that the martial arts had become a "thing," and were no longer a useful tool or art for enhancing my life in the real world.

Somehow, through meeting you and listening to what you were trying to get through to me, I finally began to get back to reality. I finally realized what a dangerous trap I was building for myself. I was really lucky, so lucky that everything worked out as it did before something really tragic happened. I had forgotten that the original combat methods as developed by our ancestors were a means of handling danger as a last resort. I was relying on physicalness and physical thinking way too much as a first resort. I had forgotten common sense. Real self-protection can more often than not be handled successfully by using our brains, thinking rationally, speaking effectively, not just leaping into dangerous areas.

Well, I made it through that dangerous stage without being hurt or killed. Fortunately, my lessons were all in the realm of manageable fighting confrontations. I could handle everything with blows and throws. I had to take some hits along the way, too, of course, but it all worked out to my benefit, I guess. Boy, that was stupid. I completely forgot about real world concepts of self-protection. I forgot to use my brains. Everything summoned up a physical-world-battle response on my part.

Maybe we should discuss the ninja arts' philosophies concerning the truth of actual life or death self-preservation combat.

I agree with you that too many trusted instructors in the United States and Europe have lost sight of that reality. Unknowingly, they have ignored the reality of the potential horror and white-washed the whole thing into an amusing recreational pastime.

MH: This past summer in America, I got to meet several interesting men who had been involved with real combat. One had been an underground operative in Afghanistan. He had practiced karate for many years, and was highly skilled. He seemed happy to see the way I move and to learn of my attitude toward daily life, all without the two of us actually having to fight

I have experienced all of the popular Japanese martial arts myself, but I wanted to find a true fighting art. I was searching for an art unlimited by any rules, and yet molded in the influence of what could be described as the most dreadful and horrifying rules imaginable. Those who claim that they know my art are funny, aren't they? I have to say this to those people: I move without even me *knowing how I do what I do.*

one another to get the message across. He commented that my techniques were hard to describe, but he thought they were wonderful. He was a happy person, and he respected me. I respect him as well. Perhaps it is because we both understand something that we do not know. This means we both are *omono*, "great beings."

I don't care whether he ever learns my ninjutsu or not. He doesn't have to learn my art. I respect those who have the kind of feeling I'm describing, no matter what their formal martial arts backgrounds may be. We share the same thing. It is not a matter of technique or speed or methods. Nothing like that. It is not a matter of a person's skill. What is important for a human being like that is the fact that he survived many actual fights. Therein lies the most important thing.

In Albuquerque, I was asked to demonstrate some of my techniques at an important anti-terrorist security training facility. They were only interested in things that would work, things that had been tried and verified through actual application. Really, they wanted that assurance more than the mechanics of my technique.

When I visited the police academy in Los Angeles, the instructor there held a fourth-degree black belt in judo. He was a remarkable man. We had a coordinator there with our film crew, and he tried to arrange for me to show the police instructors some examples of our method. There was some kind of legal touchiness that they tried to explain to me as the reason why we could not actually train together.

SKH: I run into that all the time myself. What it boils down to is the fact that the American police and military units do not want it to get out that their members were trained in what the public believes to be some sort of oriental assassination method. So to avoid potential legal hassles and public relations difficulties, they have to miss out on what we have to offer.

MH: Well, we got around that by working with our own students. They showed us examples of their technique, then I used Nagato-san and Oguri-san to demonstrate some of my techniques. I showed them all kinds of things. They seemed especially to appreciate my gun disarm techniques. That instructor was very happy to see what we practiced, and he made a remarkable comment. He said that since he could not do what I showed, he could not teach his students what he had seen. I then knew that the man had eyes. This is the most important attitude for those involved in martial arts. You may try to teach, but you cannot teach a lie. If it were not like this, then he would be teaching incorrectly and those who study with him would end up dead in a real street confrontation. It is so important to know what real fighting is, and therefore, I point out that what I have to offer is all *jisengata*, real fighting methods.

SKH: You know, I feel that your art is often misunderstood by people who visit the public training in Japan or read your interviews. There is this growing misconception that when you talk about your "art," you are leaving behind street-reality combat.

MH: In public, I rarely emphasize all this talk about real fighting. It's too much. However, when talking like this privately, Hayes-san, I can acknowledge what real fighting technique is all about. Those who claim that they know my art are funny, aren't they? That's impossible. Those people are not "all there." I have to say this to those people: I move without even *me* knowing how I do what I do.

If I had tried to know just when you were punching me from behind that time in Ohio, there is no way I could have avoided your punch. Since I did not know, *I* did not avoid it. It was as though my divine guardian spirit pulled me aside. I don't pretend that I myself avoided it.

It is very important to acknowledge that this is not a trick we are discussing here. If you think that you can avoid an unseen punch from behind by means of your own elevated skills, you might start feeling too good about it, too proud of it. The more often you play with this to impress yourself or others, the more likely it will be that you will eventually fail. You are bound to be knocked out sometime.

SKH: That's what I meant by turning martial arts training into a thing in and of itself. There are now some Americans who are fond of bragging about how well they have passed your sword test. Their own insecurities even force them to challenge their students to hit them from behind. That's digging their own grave. I mean, someday that sword is not going to come down from behind like it's supposed to. It's going to get shoved somewhere else as a total surprise.

MH: At a most crucial time, with the truest of hearts, without any preconceived motivations, I felt that taking your punch from behind was the best way of teaching the answer to your question, Hayes-san. That's why I did what I did. I was not concerned with myself. It was not like that. I appreciate, however, what you said about your feeling that I was taking the supreme risk just for the sake of your development. But it was nowhere near that complex. Out of this simple mind, I teach the way I teach. Enlightenment is at your feet.

This is the nature of the gambler, I suppose. Chances are taken because there seems to be no other way. It is automatic. It is just that way, a part of the way things must be done. So in a way, my students have to suffer because I change so often. But it just has to be that way.

A friend of mine, a Japanese sword teacher who lives in New York, commented in a letter that I am so natural and so innocently simple. But it is not really that easy. It's not that simple. He may be missing a lot of things that he could learn from me. I think that the clan of those who would lead their lives sharing the common bond of enduring the hardships of the martial path, even though there may be some quarrels among them as individuals, will be an enjoyable and rewarding and important experience. Those who lose touch with that common bond and drift off, well, I feel sorry for them.

SKH: Where do you suggest your students begin when taking on what it is that you have to teach?

MH: At the San Francisco training convention, I told you that your students still hadn't gotten the *kihon happo*, the basics. Let me tell you what I meant by that. I did not mean to sound critical

I like to give lessons by means of bawdy examples, because that always brings a laugh from people. Laughing is wonderful really. Laughter is the symbol of the winner.

of you or to insult you. The fundamentals, for example the *kata* training exercise *Koku*, must eventually be seen as the source for eight more technique exercises. *Happo*, or "eight ways," is an idiom in the Japanese language meaning "all directions." It is not the simple, literal "eight."

By using the idiom for eight directions or eight ways, I mean that each technique has to be the source for an infinite collection of possibilities. I did not at all mean to say that you or your students cannot do the basic techniques. You can all do the *kihon happo*, the ones you see in books, quite well. But each one technique has to develop into eight or more techniques. It is not enough to simply be able to do the set *kata* examples.

I am mentioning this now because it is something that I have recently started to emphasize. Since it is a recent emphasis, there is no way you could have picked it up in your early years of training with me. It's not something you could help. But there's an even more important lesson. You had questions about things you weren't sure of, and you lived and struggled with them silently. You put up with it. Days and weeks passed, and now here I am giving you answers you needed.

I would not be teaching you if you did not have that kind of ability to persevere and endure, Hayes-san. If you do not have the ability to endure, you will easily be trapped by your enemy. An enemy will taunt you and you will become angry. You will be ensnared by the enemy's tactics that way. When you do not get angry, even though your enemy attempts to make you angry, that makes your enemy angry, and leads to your winning. That is also a part of the lessons to be gotten from the *kihon happo* fundamental techniques.

RH: So that could be referred to as the psychological aspect of the *kihon happo*?

MH: Yes, that's right. That is what we call *seishin teki kyoyo* (the quality of having a clear and pure heart). Very few people will ever be able to learn this, even though you try your best to teach them. It is up to the individual's own inherent personal quality. So that's why I say that there will be many people who will simply fade out. Yes, those people will just disappear. Indeed, if it is a matter of what is inherent in one's nature, it must be admitted that enduring or persevering is not something that can be learned. It has to come naturally.

In the Heian era (794–1184), they used the word *taeiru* to mean "disappear." *Taeiru* is the same as *kieiru*, or "lose consciousness" or "faint." In the Heian period, they used the word *taeiru* poetically to indicate "fainting." It was also a poetic euphemism for sexual climax in novels of the time. The word stood for ecstasy, which hints at its *mikkyo* sexual symbolism.

I like to give lessons by means of bawdy examples, because that always brings a laugh from people. Laughing is wonderful, really. Laughter is the symbol of the winner.

Amaterasu Omikami, the sun goddess credited with the original creation of Japan, hid herself in a cave on Togakure Mountain's *Amano Iwato*. According to the legend, everyone was desperate to get her out again. Finally, after all other strategies had failed, Ameno Uzumenomikoto stripped naked and danced wildly in front of the cave. Everyone roared with laughter. There in the darkness of the cave, those peals of ringing laughter sounded like the sign of a victory. Therefore, upon hearing this, the curious Amaterasu Omikami emerged once again.

This is my way of interpreting the legend, of course. You know, I did not really have to get a university education, because I could always find my own way of interpreting things. (Laughter.)

SKH: What does a university diploma in comic relief look like?

MH: Maybe that's why the Dalai Lama of Tibet gave you this scarf for me. I am a *seijin* ("sexy guy"), and the Dalai Lama is a *seijin* ("holy man"). [It's all in how the word is written in Japanese.]

SKH: Here is one I've wanted to ask for a long time. Do you remember that opening night of the Shadows of Iga Ninja Festival in 1982, when we sneaked up from behind the crowd to announce your arrival? Anyway, that night was a real eye-opener for me. Our driver pulled up behind the crowd, and you mentioned that a car like a Cadillac Fleetwood would probably have automatic interior lights that would come on when our rear

passenger doors were opened. I hadn't thought of that giving us away, but you did.

Walking up behind the crowd, you carefully positioned the two of us so that the Festival attendees were looking into the moon as we moved through the clearing. That way, nobody saw us. We moved with a specific pace and walking method that you showed me right there on the spot. I had rarely ever seen you do any night-stalking work like that together with students before. We had only talked about these things before, you and I. Some of my seniors in Japan had showed me things, but you and I had rarely worked on that kind of training together personally.

Years later, I was speaking with some of the other senior practitioners in Japan, and I told them about that night at the Ninja Festival. Some of them were surprised to hear it. It was as though they were unsure of all that you know about what some people call the dark side of ninjutsu, the stealth and espionage work. They seemed shocked that you were teaching those things to me. All they had seen in the dojo was unarmed fighting, or ninja weapons techniques.

You have so much knowledge beyond what we usually see in the training hall. Do you keep track of or even care just who has learned what?

MH: Well, that sort of training comes up as situations require me to reveal bits of knowledge like that. If we are doing a television show, for example, I will tell the students things like that as a natural part of the activity. However, if pieces of information like that are not necessary at the moment, I will not mention it. Remember, what you learn in the dojo is just a small part of our ninjutsu legacy; dojo training can only cover the mere fundamentals.

There is no safer place than the dojo. Therefore, the students have to go outside the training hall to discover things for themselves, rather than always relying on being taught. I can only teach that approach, that feeling, that special sense. That's all I can teach, ultimately. So it could be said that I can perhaps teach you to be your own teacher.

This is really the important lesson to be gained. The common sense that human beings have is not always right. So when my students take action confidently thinking that they are following common sense, I will purposely interfere. True common sense does exist, but it exists at some other level, something beyond common common sense. Search for this kind of common sense and use it to temper your actions. Discover this ultimate common sense. I know this sounds very difficult, but as you work diligently at your *shugyo* (training leading to mastery through self-transformation), you will come to an understanding.

Here's an example. The way I see it, up to fourth-degree black belt, common sense will make sense. But after the fifth *dan*, you don't need to rely on common sense. You go beyond it. By the same token, you do not need to work at avoiding or violating common sense, either. If you try to avoid the *godan* sword by relying on your common sense, you won't succeed. You cannot avoid it by trying to rely on a deliberate lack of common sense either.

Certainly, avoiding the sword is a rather uncommon act because you do not have eyes in the back of your head. I stand behind you and bring the sword down at your head while you wait in the *seiza* kneeling position. When I attacked you from behind for your *godan* test, Hayes-san, I would imagine that you avoided the sword without thinking anything. That is usually the common thing that happens. Of course, my action of cutting a person from behind must be termed an uncommon action as well. So another meaning of the fifth degree test is that both parties reach a sort of agreement through an experience of uncommon actions. It is a body communication between the two of us.

RH: That's why you are the only one to administer the fifth-degree black belt test?

MH: It is crucial that the student and I believe in each other.

That is the kind of connection I am looking for in that *godan* test. That is the realm of the fifth level, of moving beyond the fundamental four. *Godan* is a mirror of *satori*, or enlightenment [based on a play on words in which the right portion of the Japanese written kanji character for *satori* is pronounced *go*, just as in godan, or fifth degree]. I call it the *dan* of enlightenment. When you think about it that way, you may realize slowly that the *godan* test is a very splendid and human experience, as opposed to an animalistic survival thing. When I give that test, I am not joking.

As the years have passed, you have developed to the point where this kind of talk makes sense to you. You have matured as a warrior, so we can speak like this. That in itself is wonderful to me.

SKH: At that same '82 Shadows of Iga Ninja Festival, some of the students were doing a demonstration of a building infiltration method. Using a police SWAT technique, they rappelled up and down a brick wall to get into a third-story window. You smiled and applauded with the rest of the crowd, but later in private you mentioned that the technique they used was incorrect. I was shocked to hear that. I thought if the SWAT teams relied on it, it must be effective. I was stunned to think that there could be something ineffective about a tried-and-true police method.

Similar scenes played themselves out after that one. I finally became unsure of anything unless I got it directly from you personally. I would read supposedly reliable books on military tactics and so forth, but it was never the same after that festival. I could never again be sure that this kind of misguided assumption would not happen in the future again.

MH: That's alright. That's fine. Never hesitate to try out unashamedly whatever you believe might be right. We humans learn through trial and error. You will come closer and closer to the ninja's true ways the more you explore around. And also bear in mind that it is possible that under certain circumstances a ninja might use the same kind of climbing method you were demonstrating that night. There is never any absolute.

RH: So are you saying that by exploring on our own, we can eventually approach the *kanjin kaname* (true essential experience) of the ninja's way of doing things?

MH: Yes, certainly. So first of all, if you ever have any questions, ask me. There will be no way for you to make a mistake if you ask me first, before publicly demonstrating your findings.

As I said before, the average person's common sense may be completely opposite of the ninja's common sense.

For example, that climbing method, the SWAT team technique that you used, is so highly visible. With your feet on the wall and your shoulders leaning back as you keep pressure on the rope, you create a stable climbing method but you also make quite a target. The ninja wall-scaling method requires a low profile. The ninja has to be invisible.

SKH: Sure. Sure, that makes sense. The SWAT man *is* the good guy. He has other policemen to back him up; he has sharpshooters to cover him. It's his job to be going up or down that wall for the sake of the community he has sworn to protect, so he does not need to be invisible to people outside the building. The ninja, on the other hand, would usually be in a situation where he would be called the bad guy, even if he were a police investigator doing covert intelligence-gathering work. He would have to be invisible to people outside the building as well as to people inside.

MH: The ninja might of course use somebody to climb ahead of them very visibly, and while the enemy has his eyes on that first climber, the ninja could slip in unseen at a different place. A ninja is not limited to using only one given climbing technique. To use another climber as a distraction is very much in the spirit of our ninjutsu. Still, to the others, it would indeed look like the ninja himself had done the visible climbing. That is ninjutsu, too. That is the message of the lesson I wanted to get to you at that time.

RH: So a good ninja climbing method is?

MH: Of course there are differing levels of climbing skills. That goes without saying. Anyway, if you climb vertically, there will be a space between the rope and the wall. Turn your body to the side and keep your back to the wall as you climb. That way you can keep your eyes out for enemies that might come upon you. You could endanger yourself by turning your back and looking into the shadows of the wall only.

RH: Takamatsu-sensei taught you this sort of thing?

MH: Of course, of course. We would talk over tea, or he would show me a technique when it was needed, when it came up naturally. Since there is so much to this art, I can teach certain aspects only if and when the time and place are appropriate. How do you teach mountain forest survival in the city? So in reverse, I want students to have to ferret out information from me. They will have to make a point of being where the training is, as much of the time as possible.

What if you notice that a wild boar is running right at you at full speed? Don't worry about it. Just step behind a tree and look down at him with bored contempt. It's easy for you to do this because the boar only knows one way of doing things.

RH: Some people say that you do not teach things like that until the student reaches a certain level.

MH: I don't think that's the case. However, if the student is not at an appropriate skill development level, what I could teach him might cause him to injure himself. It's useless to try to teach babies to walk properly when they can barely crawl. It's the same thing.

SKH: Before coming to Japan this fall, I met some people who alluded to connections with the Tibetan resistance movement in India. Learning of my background in ninjutsu training, they asked me what suggestions my tradition would have for them, philosophically or technically, in regard to securing freedom for their homeland. Tibet, for me, is like a "ninja workshop," in that the situation there parallels the oppression experienced by the historical ninja families of Iga so long ago. My question is what would you have said had you been there instead of me?

MH: What did you tell them?

SKH: Well, I would really rather hear what you would have said.

MH: Have faith in their gods.

SKH: That's exactly what I said! I suggested that perhaps those divine powers had some guidance for them. I must admit, though, that it was impossible for me to tell whether the resistance was the resistance, or perhaps really an informer or spy. That's all I would need, to be shot to death in India because I was "exploring the application of my training material." This is not the dojo we are talking about here. I don't know enough of the total story of the Tibetans' situation to be of any value to a resistance movement, if there even is one.

MH: Very wise. Absolutely. If you do not know who you are talking to, you could easily end up killed.

RH: What suggestions do you have for knowing how to make decisions like that?

MH: Takamatsu-sensei once told me this story. What if you notice that a wild boar is running right at you at full speed? Don't worry about it. Just step behind a tree and look down at him with bored contempt. It's easy for you to do this because the boar only knows one way of doing things. The only course that he can take, whether the road leads to hell or not, is the one that he has already taken. He has no idea of what awaits him. He sees all through the eyes of a beast. A human being walks on the road and he can see whether the road connects with other roads or not. A human being knows how to avoid something dangerous. He can conceal himself somewhere to avoid danger. After the danger passes, he takes to the road again. But the boar cannot do things like this. He is powerful, but there is helplessness in his power. This is an important lesson in life.

SKH: In movies and comic books, we always see the ninja sneaking around in black jumpsuits and masks. I do not think that you feel that is the true image of the historical ninja. Where do you think that image came from?

MH: Let me give you Takamatsu-sensei's story of the development of the ninja's image. The original ninja were Japanese warriors who ended up on the losing side of the battle. Because of the outcome of a battle, they were forced to flee to the mountains in exile.

I know that you are familiar with the history of the Togakure ninjutsu ryu. Shima Kosanta Minamoto no Kanesada, when he was sixteen years old, was a retainer (samurai) of Kiso Yoshinaka. Yoshinaka was defeated in battle at Awazu in the late 1100s. Shima Kosanta was badly injured, and fled to a mountainous area. He was *kosho* rank. He was not afraid to die, but to follow the wishes of Yoshinaka faithfully he fled the battlefield.

For example, after Yoshinaka's death, someone had to maintain the grave of this slain leader. Someone had to protect the family of Yoshinaka. He also had to let the world know the true story of the righteousness of Yoshinaka. There were many more duties as well.

In the heat of war, it is difficult to tell which side is right and which is wrong. That is the misfortune of both sides. But the victor will always have the chance to tell the public that they were the right ones. The victor's side of the story, his version of the conflict, is the one that will go down in history. The victors are the ones who write the history books. Since the legacy of ninjutsu was born from vanquished people, it was therefore not spoken highly of in the victors' historical accounts.

The Tachikawa Bunko series of ninja novels, which came out in the Taisho era (1912–1926), treated ninjutsu as something remarkable, something somewhat positive. They were, however, usually light and humorous accounts. For example, the story of Sarutobi Sasuke was told in a very lighthearted way. But in those stories written before Taisho, for example in the Edo period (1603-1867), and in *kabuki* theater performances, ninja were portrayed more as thieves.

Perhaps that is why we have this distorted image today. Also, fiction writers, not knowing the true nature of ninjutsu, played up the romanticized concepts of what they wanted ninjutsu to be for the sake of their novels. The stories that those novelists turned out dealt more with tactics of concealment, deception, and occult practices. Therefore, the modern image of ninjutsu reflects this inaccurate bias, even though I speak and write books to contradict the false stereotype. Ignorance prevails, even though an authentic practitioner of the original and true ninja art still exists today.

So from now on, you and I, Hayes-san, have to let the world know that there is a ninja like me still around today. We have a mission to accomplish, as a token of thanks to our ancestors who stretch out from a thousand years of history. We should feel we are fortunate to repay their favor. I feel that both of us should feel happy that we have evolved to the point where we are able to do this for our ancestors. We are involved and we know what ninjutsu is, and we should take pride in that fact. It is our duty to carry this art on in the true direction. We should both feel fortunate that we were born at the right time, even though both you and I have had to endure a lot of hardships and take a lot of abuse.

This is a serious topic, an important point. From the historical view, people label ninjutsu as such and such, this and that. It always relates to darkness and violence in the eyes of the uninformed. But as you realize, the truly accomplished ninja always works to avoid fighting. What do you think? We do not dwell on the thought of defeating others or sneaking up on victims in the night.

SKH: No, that has not been the point of my training. I may be capable of such things, but that is not why I train.

If you interpret ninjutsu from an animalistic or brutal survival sense, the truth is that you can end up dead with one gunshot, no matter how highly skilled you are. Even we could be killed like that. It is that easy to take a human life. Because we are human beings, however, some spark keeps us alive.

MH: I never concentrate on that either. The only thing I think about is my enjoyment. Therefore, I elevated our training legacy to the level of art. I would like to present this training legacy as an art, a humane thing, to the world.

Moreover, the truth is that America is a country of materialism. In a materialistic society, when you talk about who is stronger and who is weaker, it always comes down to the fact that the one with more material resources will be more powerful than those who have less. Comparing mechanical weapons with human limbs, the power of the unarmed is far less than that of the armed when it comes to winning and losing. If you interpret ninjutsu from an animalistic or brutal survival sense, the truth is that you can end up dead with one gunshot, no matter how highly skilled you are. Even we could be killed like that. It is that easy to take a human life. Because we are human beings, however, some spark keeps us alive. Since we are human beings, we have lived as ninja for 900 years through our humane way of approaching life. You and I are both gentlemen. People of class. This is important. Our ninjutsu is presented as an art, and I talk like an artist.

SKH: I have to say that of all the martial arts I have encountered in the world, I have only found one living art for me. All the others I worked with or explored seemed to be merely *kata*, or imitation, or sports contests. Are you ever amazed at the fact that you are the one to carry this unique phenomenon through the world for this generation? Do you ever wonder over the fact that it happened to be you?

MH: It's very simple. People like you seek me out and that reminds me of how alive I feel this art is. That's all. That's all.

It's also true that celebrities outside the art accept me as I am. Great people, recognized ones, accept me. This could be one of the surprises the art has brought to my life.

Real people are looking for other real people. Like gravitates to like. At the same time, powerful people can only associate with other powerful people. Therefore, people at the top of their worlds of endeavor seem to associate with me for their entire lives. That is mysterious to me.

For example, one of my associates is Japan's number one boat racer. Then there are the famous actors, Shinichi Chiba and Koichi Ohse, as well as other celebrities in the arts and politics. Their names are all on the invitation list for our annual birthday celebration party. Even those whom I have not seen for a long time still maintain their friendship with me. This is something for which I do feel thankful. Though I haven't seen some of them for a long time, since we dwell in the realm of space, time has no effect. Even though time passes, the connection is still there. It makes no difference. Mysterious, huh? They always love me.

But those people who do not have that much influential power or those who have not had to go through any hardships, or those who have not developed into powerful individuals, they will disappear into their own monologue. They won't listen to anyone else. There was a time that I felt all alone, but I found that as you continue to do one thing and do it well, good people keep coming around to you, one after another. They gravitate toward you, somehow. Mysterious, but true. I know that good people gravitate toward you, Hayes-san, many good high-quality people. That is the way it is supposed to be. If you are real, you attract real people.

Anywhere I go in the world, I find good friends. Maybe we can recognize a special something about one another. *Onushi dekir-una*, "You have something in you," or "There's something about you." That's a favorite line in the samurai comic strips when one dangerous warrior meets another face to face. You can pick up on a hunch like that without being told. I can often tell this. I look at a person and my sixth sense will tell me, "This one is no good." Sure, I may offer them what I can and take care of them as best I can, but I do not expect anything to come of it. After I accept them into the training hall, it's up to their quality and ability.

So as you know, I never have to tell anybody not to come back to my training hall, or anything of that nature. I've never thrown out a single soul, absolutely none in my past or present, but those who do not have the aptitude disappear by themselves nonetheless. Mysterious. It's truly mysterious.

Masaaki Hatsumi waits in a natural *shizen no kamae* posture with the *shikomi zue* cane in his right hand.

Stephen Hayes attacks with a right-fist punch. The defending Hatsumi slams down on the attacking right arm with the left-hand end of the sword cane.

The scabbard portion of the sword cane is pressed down and in, to immobilize both of Hayes's upper arms.

Using the tip of the scabbard to bar Hayes's left arm with a wrist lock, Masaaki Hatsumi presses down on the attacker's spine with the handle end of his sword.

The scabbard is removed from the sword, clearing the blade. This is an example of the *iai-nuki* (sword-drawing) *koppo* (bone-attacking) method.

The drawn blade and scabbard are used to capture the attacker's neck.

This close-up shows how Masaaki Hatsumi uses his finger to secure the blade to the scabbard for the *hasami giri* (scissor cut).

Instead of a moving blade cut, a lateral body swing cuts the arteries of the left side of the neck, disguising Hatsumi's action from view.

The sword is further drawn into position to pierce downward into the attacker's left lung.

This technique demonstrates the closeness of *hanbojutsu* methods and the sword arts, and suggests that the roots of sword combat lie in the history of stick fighting.

Masaaki Hatsumi waits for the attacker with his concealed blade in position in front of his thighs.

Stephen Hayes initiates a right-hand punching attack, and Masaaki Hatsumi absorbs the attack lightly.

Immediately, the attacker continues with a left punch. Hatsumi catches Hayes's left hand, hitting his left elbow with the *shikomi zue*, forcing the attacker forward.

Defender Hatsumi positions his attacker's hand on his left thigh and crushes down with the sword cane.

Masaaki Hatsumi secures the scabbard with his right hand while applying a *gyakute waza* (wrist twist) to the attacker's left arm. He simultaneously draws the blade from its scabbard.

The defender places the blade edge on the back of the attacker's neck, and uses his levering scabbard to deliver push-pull cutting pressure. Notice that Masaaki Hatsumi's right leg is ready to kick at any time.

There is no safer place than the dojo. Therefore, the students have to go outside the training hall to discover things for themselves, rather than always relying on being taught. I can only teach that approach, that feeling, that special sense. That's all I can teach, ultimately. So it could be said that I can perhaps teach you to be your own teacher.

Masaaki Hatsumi waits in a natural pose with the sword cane gripped in both hands.

Stephen Hayes attacks with a right-hand strike, which is struck out of the air by Hatsumi's cane tip. While countering the attacker's right arm, the defender is directing his attention to the attacker's left fist.

Hatsumi avoids the immediate left follow-up attack by shifting to the left of the attacker as he moves.

The attacker's fist and body are allowed to continue forward, and the blade is drawn in such a way to permit the attacker's momentum to provide the cutting power. As he applies the cut, Masaaki Hatsumi's right leg provides checking cover to the attacker's left leg.

As Stephen Hayes continues forward, Hatsumi quickly drops his right sword-gripping hand below Hayes's right wrist to exert a twisting leverage cut.

Masaaki Hatsumi waits in *otonashi no kamae* with his sword cane held in both hands behind the body.

Defender Hatsumi twists to his left to receive attacker Hayes's right punch with the rising tip of the cane. This movement also jams the attacker's potential left-hand follow-up punch.

Leaving the cane jammed in place, Hatsumi uses his left hand to pull the blade from its scabbard.

Masaaki Hatsumi uses the scabbard to apply leverage while piercing through to the opposite side of the attacker's neck.

With a full body drop, defender Hatsumi uses his right forearm on the back of his blade to cut and redirect his attacker's body.

Masaaki Hatsumi releases the scabbard and pulls his sword to his shoulder.

Both hands are then used to apply a cut to the attacker's neck.

4
BONDS AND HARDSHIPS

I slowly allow my ankles to slide further apart. The muscles along the insides of my thighs relax and my torso lowers into a full sideways split. I reach out along the worn black canvas of my ninjutsu *dogi* trouser legs and grasp the outside edges of my cotton-soled *tabi* (split-toed shoe–socks). Tightening my arms slightly, I pull my chest forward and down toward the pale green tatami matting that covers the floor. Amused at the contradiction played out by my body, I "work at relaxing" the muscles of my back and hips, lowering inch by inch the crossed lapels of my black training jacket.

From out of the blackness of the night outside, other training members continue to appear and trickle into the paneled training area of the Bujinkan Someya dojo. Koichi Oguri has ridden the trains all the way down from Tochigi Prefecture, just as he has done for all the years I have known him. The muscular Toshiro Nagato has driven his Toyota Land Cruiser for hours across the metropolis of Tokyo. Major Fumio Manaka has a rare evening free from his duties with the Japanese Land Self-Defense Forces, and is able to attend the training tonight. Kikkoman Soy Sauce Company executive Yukio Noguchi and Isamu Shiraishi enter the dojo together.

We are all here for the twice-weekly senior instructors' training
session with Hatsumi-sensei. Training sessions with the grandmaster float from dojo to dojo, depending on the night of the week.
Some nights we train here at Kenichi Someya's dojo. Other nights
are usually spent at Tetsuji Ishizuka's Kashiwa City training hall.
Tomorrow night Rumiko and I will go for a private training
session with Dr. Hatsumi at the dojo of Isamu Shiraishi. Ironically, Togakure ryu ninjutsu 34th generation grandmaster Masaaki Hatsumi does not have a dojo of his own, and therefore
divides his teaching time among the dojos of several of his
students who live in the Noda City area.

I cannot help but experience a fleeting notion of nostalgia,
looking up from the floor at these men who stretch, laugh, and
converse around me. Now into our second decade of warrior
training together, these were the ones who first took me in as a
fellow crazy seeking out the forbidden, and then secret, arts of the
ninja all those years ago before anyone even suspected the ninja
craze of the 1980s. It all seems so different now, when I think back
to the early days of Hatsumi's Bujinkan dojo. In those years
immediately following the death of 33rd grandmaster Toshitsugu
Takamatsu, there were no ninjutsu dojos in the world except for
the back room of the home of Masaaki Hatsumi.

None of us here tonight were called "master instructor" in those
days, either. We were merely the ones who trained; bold and
fearless and foolish guinea pigs for his technique experimenta-
tions. His methods were murderous, applied with way too much
force for civilized training, leaving us bruised and often limping,
but our reward was the opportunity to take home the personal
experience of a unique form of knowledge that had been handed
down from one master to the next for thirty-four generations of
Japanese history.

Masaaki Hatsumi moves into position kneeling in front of the
kamiza (spiritual center) of the dojo. There high up on the eastern
wall of the training hall is the shelf with its miniature shrine
structure. Clipped *sakaki* cleyera boughs fill vases on both ends of
the shelf, and portraits of Hatsumi and Takamatsu look down on
the dojo from positions just to the left and right of the sacred
miniature platform. We all line up in rows across the dojo, in
position behind the grandmaster.

I look up and down the rows. There are twenty-three people
here tonight, all of whom carry the *shidoshi-ho* (instructor),

shidoshi (senior instructor), or *shihan* (master instructor) title. I think back to the early days of my apprenticeship in the home of Hatsumi-sensei, when there were no more than eighteen of us in Japan practicing the art of ninjutsu. We would all crowd into the little *hachijo* (8-mat room) that was our dojo then, and take turns kicking and throwing each other around the 12-foot square space.

The grandmaster brings his hands together in front of his chest and begins the recitation of a barely audible mantric pledge for safe and spirited training under the watchful influence of the lineage's *bujin*, or "warrior guardian spirit." The grandmaster then weaves his fingers into a quick succession of *ketsu-in* (energy-channelling hand posturings), makes the invisible cuts with the sword of his spirit's intention, and roars out the opening pledge.

"Shikin haramitsu daikomyo!"

We all follow his lead with our own shout. *Shikin haramitsu daikomyo!* ("Every experience we encounter carries within it the potential for the breakthrough to enlightened consciousness we seek.") Hands clap sharply twice, a bow of acknowledgment is performed, one more sharp clap and follow-up bow, and the grandmaster turns to face us.

"Onegai shimas," we bow in request for training.

Hatsumi-sensei looks down the line of instructors and his eyes lock with mine for a brief moment. He begins a brief lecture comparing the emperor's triple symbol of mirror, sword, and jeweled pendant, with the training structure of his ninja dojo. Our taijutsu is like a mirror of our inner feelings. Freedom of movement is not possible without a corresponding freedom of the spirit. Our *shinobi gatana* and *hanbo* are compared with the sword symbol, and our *kusarifundo* is compared with the emperor's symbolic pendant. As symbols, the three should remind us of what is our right and our potential for realization, if only we are strong enough to stay with the training and overcome all the obstacles and hardships.

We bow once more and the training begins. Bodies twist, tumble, and flow with the example techniques provided by the grandmaster of the art. We all work at capturing the essence of Hatsumi's movement, but this is clearly his show. His energy is free and spontaneous whereas ours is but a reflection of the elusive fluidity that characterizes the effortless combat method of Toratsugu, the tiger of the Togakure legacy. His coaching is an urgent blend of direct instruction, clipped comments identifying points of the action missed by the student, and jubilant encouragement.

He laughs out loud as Rumiko's heel discretely slips behind mine and she throws me to the floor at the exact moment when I had expected her to succumb to my strangulation attack. She goes on to find a new training partner, and the grandmaster takes me aside conspiratorially to show me a secret counter to the counter to the technique he had given us all to practice. Hours pass like minutes, and we are stunned to look up at the clock when our teacher announces that the night's training has at last drawn to a close.

We bow our acknowledgment to the shelf full of symbols that mutely remind us all of the significance, the history, and the power behind our lineage. We bow our acknowledgment of gratitude to the grandmaster, head of our lineage and mentor to each of us as individual aspirants on the razor-edged path leading to the warrior's attainment of the universal secrets.

A low-standing portable table, just thirteen inches high, is produced, unfolded, and loaded with fruit, rice crackers, and cups of hot Japanese *ocha* tea. Some of the training members sit cross-legged at the table in their black training suits, the backs of the heavy jackets still soaked through with perspiration. Others emerge from a tiny dressing area, tucking in shirttails and pulling on street jackets, to join the grandmaster's conversation at the table. After some light preparatory conversation with the small crowd in attendance, Masaaki Hatsumi hands me an orange and indicates that Rumiko should again turn on the tape recorder that has followed us throughout our day. One by one the training members bow their goodnights to leave for home, and the grandmaster's story continues.

MH: Because you and I both have grown up during our years together, Hayes-san, we can now converse frankly like this. We have grown up and gone through the seasoning process together, you and I, as martial artists. I thank you, Rumiko-san. You had a hard time, too. You didn't know the first word about martial arts, but since you loved Stephen, you did your best.

SKH: Actually, Rumiko is now a much better student than I am. Whatever you tell her to train on, she goes and does it without question. I always have to examine it and look for the hidden

traps or loopholes, figure it out myself and then finally get around to doing whatever it was that you told me I needed to do all along.

MH: People say that the women from Kyushu make the best wives. They are strong and they respect their men. You married well, Hayes-san.

I know that the two of you have had to put up with a lot of hardship and heartbreak since the time you left Japan to move back to your home in America. For a person who is striving to master any discipline, martial or otherwise, hardships and toil are inevitable along the path. But to the warrior who belongs on the path, that hardship does not mean much; he does not even think of it as hardship. Hardship and trial are the very means to growing stronger, to becoming invincible.

Therefore, I say that the *ku* in *kuro* (hardship, heartache) will lead to *kuji* ("nine syllables," a ninja spiritual power method). The *ku* character of *kuro* means suffering. That suffering will produce the strength that empowers your *kuji*. By forging on through hardship, you come to know the overwhelming quality of willpower that enables your intentions to become reality. Of course you realize that what we are talking about here is different from ordinary *kuji*.

After you have endured all the hardships, you will transcend this *kuji* and go on to to the elevated realization of *juji* ["tenth syllable," a ninja spiritual power method]. *Ju* of *juji* [crossing his fingers one over the other] represents the coming together of male

and female in the teachings of *mikkyo* ["secret doctrines,"
esoteric Buddhist knowledge]. It means love. It creates the basis
for safety, prosperity, and welfare for future generations.

Only those who have grown through hardship will be able to
identify with others who share the common bond of having
experienced this kind of development of power. That is the true
state or nature of *kuji* and *juji*. This is the meaning behind *mikkyo*
as we experience it. It is also the meaning behind *budo* (martial
arts).

There it is. Those who do not share this common bond of
experiencing the overcoming of hardship will be utterly destroyed
by this process of attempting to develop the spiritual powers of
juji.

There is a saying, "Even if you are granted the powers of *kuji*,
you are not necessarily granted those of *juji*." You may be united
with this momentum of trial and accomplishment at the *kuji* level,
but without knowing it, you may accidentally profane something
that is god-given, like love or a special bond that was in your fate
to cultivate rather than weaken. Those persons not only will be
demolished, but will demolish others with them as well. I think
that is the crucial part of this teaching.

Even in religious traditions, it is stated that once you get
married, you should not split the marriage up. Perhaps some of
the roots of this concept I am talking about are found in that
religious teaching. Be careful of taking higher connections in life
in a way that reduces them to the trivial. That is dangerous, a
deadly mistake, both spiritually and physically.

Hayes-san, as the top in what you are doing in your country, I
am sure that you have had to endure all kinds of hardship. When
I came to America five years ago, you were doing a very good job.
Since then, as we discussed previously, some of your students left
you, didn't they? They went away and out on their own?

SKH: Yes. But I suppose that was inevitable. Personalities are
different. People have different needs. Perhaps they felt that I was
not addressing their unique needs.

MH: But some of these people are still involved in the martial
arts, aren't they?

SKH: Some are. Some are even highly ranked teachers of the
Bujinkan dojo method now. I didn't give them those grades, of
course, but you did or one of the other senior instructors over here
did. Since these people were practitioners of ninjutsu . . .

MH: You're saying that in past tense.

SKH: Well, . . .

RH: A lot of them maintain their reputations as ninjutsu practitioners, even though they are no longer training with the rest of us. Since they were at one time students of Stephen Hayes, the public considers them as still associated with Stephen Hayes and our Shadows of Iga Ninja Society. Therefore, they can still run dojos or hold seminars and people will come for training.

MH: That's it. The name. That's what is important, isn't it? People say that they learned the art from Dr. Hatsumi. People then say that they separated from Dr. Hatsumi. This means that both you and I must be regarded highly by society, if our names mean that much. These incomplete students, the ones you were referring to before, they can't do anything. When you look at that student's technique or movement, you can tell that he can't do our method.

RH: Stephen himself admits that he did not teach some of those early students the art very well. Since Stephen himself was still working on fully understanding all that this art was in the early days, and some of those persons were students in those early years of ninjutsu in America, they only got small bits of inaccurate information whenever Stephen made short visits back to the United States.

MH: It was the same for me. Exactly the same. It takes so long to develop fully. From this September 21st, you and I are the same, Hayes-san. On September 21st, at the time of taking the name of Toratsugu, I felt that I had become the full embodiment of the role of *soke*. At the same time, you were awarded your seventh-degree black belt under the certification of Toratsugu. I know that you can teach the true methods of ninjutsu in America. The time has come. I want you to know that you should present yourself proudly.

SKH: It is a tough job maintaining a reputation. There is so much misunderstanding in the Western world now about just who is a qualified teacher. It's pretty bad. Some people have even published accounts wherein you are said to have stated that even I am not qualified. Of course that is ridiculous, but it is hard to combat that sort of thing. People do not know where to turn.

MH: I am sure you will find that as you become increasingly recognized, even more people are bound to throw more stones at you. Take for example the famous Japanese Buddhist monk

I am not doing all this for my own sake. If I am unable to pass on the wisdom of our centuries-old tradition directly, if I can't get the message across personally, I would be happy if some of you could do it. I live in the hope that it will come true.

Nichiren (1222–1282). Even he had to endure stones thrown by detractors when he set out to introduce his teachings. Saicho (767–822) from Enryakuji temple on Hie Mountain was given the title of Dengyo Daishi ("great saint of transmitted knowledge") after his death. While he was alive, however, many people refused to take him and his *mikkyo* seriously. Therefore, he went through hardship, but as a result, he created the Tendai Buddhist center on Mt. Hie for later generations.

Therefore, to be blunt about the way that I live, I am not doing all this for my own sake. If I am unable to pass on the wisdom of our centuries-old tradition directly, if I can't get the message across personally, I would be happy if some of you could do it. I live in the hope that it will come true. Therefore, in order to develop strong people capable of handing on our legacy, I do not feel bad at all about subjecting you to hardship and heartbreak.

RH: We gladly go through any hardships you set up.

MH: When *shugyosha* [persons undergoing the trials of severe self-development training] talk to each other from the heart, it is often accompanied by tears. With this reality in mind, my teacher taught me the following *kuji* invocation. [Masaaki Hatsumi twists his hands together and recites a string of nine syllables.] I will teach it to you today, Hayes-san. Later tonight, I will write out the characters of the power phrase on a scroll of paper for you. [Stephen Hayes follows his teacher's actions and repeats the nine syllables several times.]

Here's a story Takamatsu-sensei told me one year before his death. "Birds and beasts will not shed tears, even though they experience the ultimate sadness. They will not shed tears even in the highest of joys. But human beings shed tears when they experience both sorrow and bliss. And this *kuji*, these special nine syllables, was born in that heightened state of awareness of life."

*T*oshitsugu Takamatsu binding his fingers to-gether in the *uchijishi no in* symbol of directed intention, strategy, and action.

Takamatsu-sensei said this *kuji* phrase was created by our ancestors looking out through the tears of preparation for death. He said, "This is our own lineage's *kuji*. It is different from that nine-syllable string usually attributed to the ninja in the books and movies. It is very important for you to know its roots." That is what he told me. That is what I hand on to you.

On September 21st, I visited the grave of Toshitsugu Taka-matsu, accompanied by thirty students. We had gone to see his widow, and in front of the grave I wrote the following oath: "On this very day of September 21, the day of *higan* [traditional Japanese grave visitation day] in the 61st year of the Showa era [1986], bearing the name of Toratsugu, having adopted the *tsugu* of Toshitsugu and the *tora* of Moko no Tora, I vow to live out the rest of my life in true fashion as the *soke* Toratsugu. I said to *live*, not merely to act a role. I am now fully confident of this." This is what I wrote and presented to my teacher.

A former student of mine went to see Takamatsu-sensei's widow and claimed that he is the one who can best carry on her late husband's martial art. His widow simply said, "Do whatever

I might have done impolite things to my students in causing them hardships. But we are martial friends, and I think that everything is understood for what it really is. Things are not taken too seriously among friends.

you want to do." He immediately went out and established his own *ryu-ha*. That is fine with me, he can do what he wants, but she had become very worried.

Whenever I went to visit his grave, I was usually accompanied by only one other person, Taguchi-san, the head of our Bujinkan training hall in Osaka. She always asked me if I had any other students. She always told Taguchi-san to be supportive of Hatsumi-sensei, because she considers me as her own son. I went there for 15 years, so sensei and his wife felt as though I were their own son, and they did not have any children of their own. She was really worried.

The other day, thirty people from my dojo showed up in front of her. She was so happy that tears filled her eyes. She said in front of those people that I was a great person. Everyone was in tears, and I remembered that particular *kuji* phrase that Takamatsu-sensei had given me. I knew that all evil obstacles would be overcome.

SKH: I can identify with those feelings in my own way. I find it disturbing, sad really, that so many weak and troubled individuals are able to get away with using your name so freely. All kinds of people now claim that you have certified them as high-ranking instructors. My students don't understand why you let those people get away with it. I tell them it has to do with my training, my becoming stronger as a warrior. Sure, it would be a lot easier if you would just state once and for all who is a legitimate teacher of your art and who is not, but then, that would take away all the hardship and its tempering effects in my life. I know that would be too easy. With that kind of air-clearing, I would no longer have to be a warrior. You would have done all my reputation establishing for me.

MH: I know that you, Hayes-san, and Rumiko went through your own hardships because of some of the things I have and have not said. But I do not feel sorry for you, because you are attaining the power of *kuji*. I think you understood the true meaning of *kuji* and *juji* today.

To show the meaning of *kuji*, I once ordered you to punch me from behind in Ohio. If I were an ordinary teacher, I would not have ordered you to do so. But I did it out of desperation. And later I realized that I was not even aware of the degree of my desperation either.

I must be a fool, huh? I say things without thinking about the seriousness of my actions. But my teacher trained me to be that way. Someone else will have a hallucination. To some people, some things become very serious, but those things are not really serious to me at all. So I can do anything without fear. It may even be a battle I am not destined to win, but I will fight on without fear. Then, as a result, I may just win after all. This is the nature I was born with as a martial artist. Takamatsu-sensei praised me. He had never seen a man with that much courage or fearlessness. But you could say that a person who has no fear is also a reckless person. (Laughing.) So it could be the same thing in reverse. Maybe it was not praise. Maybe he was accusing me of being reckless.

So up to now, I might have been a fool. I might have done impolite things to my students in causing them hardships. But we are martial friends, and I think that everything is understood for what it really is. Things are not taken too seriously among friends. From now on, you will have to do the same thing with your martial friends. It is like taking turns, passing it on. And thus this

art has survived and been handed down for nine hundred years.

At the same time, frankly speaking, I do not really enjoy the task of teaching students. It's not something I do willingly.

Soke Shinryuken Masamitsu Toda was a great teacher, a great swordsman, a master of the Bikenshin ryu sword method. He was a chief instructor for the official Tokugawa government sword school in Kyoto in the middle 1800s. When Iinaosuke was appointed to the position of *karo* (advisor to the shogun), Shinryuken suddenly resigned from his position as sword instructor. He could foresee the political difficulties that lay ahead in Japan's immediate future, based on the appointment of Iinaosuke, and he felt that it would be improper to supply his techniques to any one group of people who would only end up using them to kill or be killed for the sake of Japanese internal politics.

He did not want to provide the means for one Japanese to kill another Japanese in battle. Therefore he simply resigned as chief instructor of the government's sword school. The official historical records for the Kinki Chiho region simply note that he quit his position, but do not state any details as to why. I know the story, and can understand his feelings and motivations for making the choice he did. Therefore, both you and I have to apply self-discipline and take care of ourselves.

It is not necessarily a good thing to be famous. Indeed, from now on I have to focus on teaching my art for the benefit of the Japanese people as well as the people of the world. The most important point of the martial arts is exemplified in this story about Shinryuken Masamitsu Toda. We must do whatever we can to aid the cause of peace of mankind and freedom and happiness. To maintain a good balance among these qualities, I do what I do. Therefore, Hayes-san, you should live this art for the sake of the American people, your own community. Frankly, I do not want you to practice or teach this art for my sake. For the sake of good-hearted persons in America, I want you to teach authentic ninjutsu as a way to approach living.

Anyway, back to the *kuji* topic. But then that is *kuji*, really, isn't it?

Well, recently I was a part of a panel discussion at the Tendai Buddhist center on Mt. Hie . . .

RH: Do you have a tape from the discussion on Mt. Hie?

MH: No. It was not all that great.

You might think that you have captured the point of a technique with a camera lens, or written a description of the most important aspect of the technique, but in doing so, you have totally missed the real point, the crucial essence which is always so difficult to detect without actually being able to do it.

RH: I mean do you have a tape of just your own lecture?

MH: Even my lecture was not all that great. I had to go along with the level of the audience.

You know, I never had to study hard when I was at the university. I'm not trying to justify my behavior here. I'm just commenting on a bad aspect of Japanese education. Japanese professors extract information from books and transfer it to their own notebooks and then teach strictly from those notes. Since that was the case, I could always get away with doing something outside of the classroom and then get a copy of what was said in the lecture. Instead of paying a lot of money on transportation to school and back, I could spend it on something much more enjoyable.

SKH: Sounds like my experience at college. Never let your studies interfere with your education, I always used to say.

MH: There are so many lecturers who just bring along some notes and read them to the audience. Unfortunately, many of my fellow lecturers at Mt. Hie were of that type. I would like to tell the audience not to bother listening to that kind of lecturer. I don't take anything along with me. I just take my body. I look at the audience and I can tell what they want to hear and for what they are searching. Those who are incapable of doing that are not qualified to be giving lectures.

SKH: I guess they think that performance doesn't matter. They think of themselves as transmitting raw knowledge itself, and it is the duty of the audience to get it. I know martial arts teachers like that. They expect their students to blindly copy them.

MH: This is the media age, the age of the instant copy. But something merely copied cannot move people's hearts. Therefore,

I move in such a way that no one can copy me. Photographs cannot capture my action. Pictures are useless. I know you understand what I mean. Writing a description of the movement is also useless. You might think that you have captured the point of a technique with a camera lens, or written a description of the most important aspect of the technique, but in doing so, you have totally missed the real point, the crucial essence which is always so difficult to detect without actually being able to do it. As I always say, there is only one Picasso. In the martial arts, I am unique.

SKH: Don't you wonder what Picasso had to go through in order to become what he eventually was, I mean the learning involved long after art school was over?

MH: After returning from America on my recent trip, I promoted a few of my students to ninth dan. Little by little they are beginning to understand my message. As they progress, the more advanced they become, the more they will understand.

SKH: Which message? That completion of the formal training is really a new form of beginning?

MH: The only way to learn this art is to be willing to give up, to let go, to let go of what they may have practiced or done in the past, to give up and be willing to discard that which is no longer needed. By letting go, learning not to cling or be attached, you can attain the zero state. From that point, you will truly begin to make positive progress. There are times that you will go through hardships, and there are some times that you will feel that you have gotten tired of training. Your life will be very different, based upon your decision to hang on to the art or to drop it. When you cut yourself off from the martial arts, that's a different kind of return to zero, though.

RH: Because nothing more will be produced?

MH: Yes. Those who hang on to their martial arts training, even though they have to endure hardships or feel that they are tired of training, they realize that there is no other way to progress, and so they keep going in the art. From that point, an insight into the indescribable and elusive, a fascination with the mystery of the art, is born.

In a way, I always feel separated from what I have done. Hayes-san, you have taught many people over the years. "Time flies so fast and the people that you meet are all the same; they come into your life and then vanish." [Quote from Matsuo Basho (1644–1694), famous haiku poet from Japan's Iga area.]

There is the concept of *musha shugyo*, or travelling the warrior path. It is important to know that it is not always necessary to leave your home to experience *musha shugyo*. The challenge comes to you no matter where you are. Students will come to you and they will leave, and the cycle will repeat itself over and over again. It is just like Basho's poem. So in the beginning, you may think that to teach at your best is the greatest thing that you can do. But to do your best or to champion unwaveringly some cause—when you look at these things from the vantage point of the full length of your life—may not be that significant at all.

RH: Therefore, there are twenty years of *omote* ("front," or obvious) training and then twenty years of *ura* ("back," or less obvious) training, right?

MH: That's why what I tell my students is a way to think, rather than the way to become enlightened. Age will mature and season you. Indeed there is a saying that once you become a parent, you will know how much your own parents did for you. At the same time, as the years go on, students will change in many ways.

Animals, when they get old enough, will leave their parents and go their own way. But in the human realm, the bond between children and parents will not dissolve, though in some families these days, it seems to more resemble the animal pattern. Once an animal leaves its family, that is the end of their relationship. It is a remarkable thing in a way.

Again, that brings us back to the *godan* fifth-degree black belt test in my training hall. As we discussed before, the *godan* test is, in a way, an indication of animal-like qualities. But then fighting is also an animalistic thing. And this animal sense is a necessary thing. Once you have passed the *godan* fifth-degree test, it means you have passed the barrier of knowing what the martial arts are.

For that reason, up to fourth dan, I can only give out ranks according to the students' physical skills. For instance, some people have been involved with kung-fu or karate or other forms of the martial arts for many years. When they combine their arts with ours, the value of their own skills will increase. But to go above to the *godan*, there is a barrier that not everybody can pass through. Some stay where they are, because passing this fifth dan test is a very difficult thing. I will use my feelings alone to give out ranks up to fourth degree, however, and I don't care whatever anyone says.

SKH: The difficulty for those of us who live in the Western world is the fact that your dan rank awards are criticized for not having any meaning anymore. Some pretty weak individuals now brag of having a Masaaki Hatsumi black belt license. It really makes things awkward for those of us who are trying to maintain the purity of the art in the United States and Europe.

MH: Those words are expressed by people who have a childlike outlook, in a way. They do not know the real me. It is the same with those who do not know the real me and claim that I do not have any power to my techniques. But those who have trained with me for a long time know that there would be a disaster if I were to use my full power. When I visited America, I told the participants, "Play, just play!" I know you know why I used that word, because you know what I am, and you believe in me. If I had used my real power, as would be required in a true fight, there would have been many wounded and injured participants. I thought that would be obvious.

Sonshi [Chinese warfare theoretician Sun Tzu] said, "If you know yourself and if you know your enemy, you will win every battle." Likewise, it is proper courtesy for martial artists to know their training partners and move in an appropriate manner in accordance with what is fitting for their opponent when training together. That's the way to win in training.

Many martial artists do not seem to be aware of this courtesy, I suppose. When I went to America, I wanted to observe these courtesies in order not to appear rude. In Japan, if you visit somebody's house and fail to take off your shoes upon entering, it is considered impolite. But in the United States, I know it would be considered strange behavior to take off your shoes in your American host's house. This is all I can say. Perhaps I did something that looked strange, something that might have appeared out of place from the American people's point of view, because of the difference in courtesies or martial manners.

SKH: In my years of doing seminars in North America and Europe, I have found that I have to tune in quickly to what kind of group I am appearing before. Are they new to the art; do they have to have the art proven to them? Are they experienced somewhat; do they need to be stimulated and encouraged? Are they dedicated practitioners; do they need to be shown all the little details that they need to make the art their own? I find that the more advanced the group, the more they want the details of the basics. Ironically, new people are bored with the basics. They want to be entertained with a lot of advanced things that are fun and challenging, even though they can't do the techniques at all.

In the early days of having just returned from living in Japan, everyone at the seminars was new to the art. They had to be; no one else in America had ever been exposed to the art of ninjutsu. I myself was an unknown, so here was this unknown guy offering an unknown art. To add to the complexity, it has to be admitted that Americans are people who demand proof before they invest their faith. I had to be able to give them results, but I was involved in an art that would not permit the demonstration of how it outclassed others.

I mean, the better judo man can demonstrate why he is better on the mat against other judo men. The better boxer can always agree to demonstrate his superiority in the ring by flattening challengers. How do you do that with a fighting art that was developed for the sake of survival at all costs?

It was very difficult coming up with a seminar policy at first. I was very naive, I guess, looking back now. We just invited people in and taught them, with no concern for what would happen if someone wanted to challenge the validity of what I was teaching. It was wild sometimes. I took a pair of nunchaku sticks away from a guy once as he flailed away trying to get my head. I just acted like I knew what I was doing, slipped in there, and grabbed them away without even getting touched. One guy at a seminar, a soldier, all of a sudden tried to wrestle me to the ground to prove that what I was teaching didn't work. It was awful. Here I am being wrestled by this big leering soldier with a shaved head. He may have thought he was having fun, but I could see my budding reputation going right down the drain. I ended up deciding to punch him in the face to knock him off me. He got up, blood running out of his head, kind of staggering but grinning. *He thought it was great!* That's what he wanted to see.

I was shocked, not about the fight, but about the grim reality that here I was trying to teach people and assist them in gaining strengths and insights, and one of those people had come at me with an entirely out-of-the-blue different purpose. I was so lucky, so incredibly lucky, that I wasn't sued for everything I owned.

That's the way America works, you know. A person can do something stupid like attack a martial arts teacher as he tries to run a seminar, but he can always get the courts to somehow

When you first came to Japan all those years ago, we were in the stage of creating the original family, so each member of that original family should be respected as a founder of our tradition in the modern world. You have your own personal family of students as a part of our broader clan, Hayes-san, just as the other senior instructors have set up theirs.

punish his victim as though the victim were at fault for allowing him to be stupid.

It's tough knowing just what is good martial courtesy and what is necessary roughness on the participants to make them understand and respect how much you can do. You go a little too easy on people and they all strut away from the seminar bragging about how you don't have any power compared with them. You go a little too hard on people and they sue you for your house and your baby's college education fund. It is a tough one, that question of just what is proper martial etiquette.

MH: Perhaps I see things from a different light, now that I have entered into the senior years of my life. I am now approaching sixty. I am getting old.

RH: Oh no. You get younger as you get older.

MH: No, to tell the truth, my body is not as healthy as I would like it to be. And at the same time, you never know when you will die, and I feel happy that you have evolved to the point that you and I can talk candidly like this. This instant-to-instant awareness of the current moment is like writing a will. Takamatsu-sensei used to tell me, "Even if you find only one person that can understand and share your thoughts, that is fine."

Up to now, I would teach anybody who was enthusiastic. I taught them with my best intentions and methods. But this willingness to give to all might have been misunderstood by some people. After I went through the transformation pledge of becoming Toratsugu, I came to realize philanthropy to everyone may not be appropriate. I want to build a clan with people who share my way of thinking, people who are matured and seasoned enough to have grasped the crucial essence of this tradition. To keep this art going into the future, everybody will have to grow up, and keep up the momentum through the establishment of their own martial families.

When you first came to Japan all those years ago, we were in the stage of creating the original family, so each member of that original family should be respected as a founder of our tradition in the modern world. Now it is time for the clan to be established. It is no longer just a family, it has expanded into a clan. You have your own personal family of students as a part of our broader clan, Hayes-san, just as the other senior instructors have set up theirs.

As the head of this art, or clan of artists, I feel this is the way we should think. Therefore, in my art, only those who have moved along with me through this *kukan* (space) without hesitating to think or question can reach that ultimate goal of the warrior arts. For that reason, I say that I am a UFO. I say that I am not Japanese, I have no nationality, I am a UFO, unidentifiable and formless. The reason I say that relates to my previous comment about moving through space with me.

It may sound like I am joking around, but I am not. "I shall return," I said, when I left on that last evening of your Shadows of Iga Ninja Festival in 1982. Later, I did return. General MacArthur was a great man. The reason I chose his words was because of his insightful comment, "Old soldiers never die; they just fade away." This is a wonderful statement. The ninja is the same, the ninja is like the general. He shared our philosophy. We fade away; we do not go out with unnecessary noise and drama. I guess the ninja philosophy fits the American way of thinking, for MacArthur expressed that ninja philosophy so well.

This book is an important project. You can share this advanced training with the rest of the world for me. As I have mentioned before, I recognize how fully you have come to understand the path of living as a martial artist. It is not a deep concept. It is simple and natural.

RH: It may be a natural thing, but when it comes from you, it sounds so much more impressive.

MH: It is only natural, but when a person is growing up there will be worldly desire, and natural things can sometimes take on a light of exaggerated importance. When a person is doing his best—as much as he can—some unnoticed negative points may develop. For example, my teacher used to tell me, "A puppy is so happy when it plays with its master. He excitedly hangs onto his master's leg, but his paws are dirty. This could be seen in a happy light, but you realize that your pants will get dirty." I thought that made a lot of sense.

Takamatsu-sensei used a puppy to describe a person with full enthusiasm. That person may think that he is doing his best, but there may be some mistakes that he is committing without knowing it. His superiors will keep in touch with what he is doing wrong, by simply watching him. He must discover for himself what he is doing wrong.

Everyone goes through this same process. Look at the mother and child relationship. When a child misbehaves, the mother scolds him. But she will not continue to hold a grudge against her own child. It is over when the child soon realizes that he was wrong. A mother might even get angry when her children do not listen to her, but there is no hatred nor manipulative power-wielding in the mother and child relationship. The scolding comes from the true sincerity of her heart. And a child will not hold it against his mother forever. So too in the martial arts, those who share the common bond will feel the same as in the mother–child relationship. The juniors appreciate the seniors for their patient guidance. I know this is true.

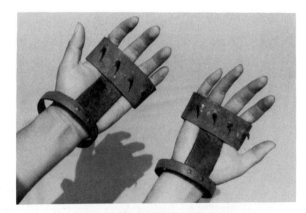

Shuko hand claws; *shuko* and *ashiko* foot claws.

The reason that the ninja was able to render his body invisible was because he had attained the *gokui* (ultimate essence) of *ninpo taijutsu*. The first secret tool on any list of the ninja's arsenal should be the hand and foot claws. The teachings of our ninja legacy admonish us not to seek out enemies, but rather to avoid having to deal with them. The fighting posture that best embodies this teaching is *hicho no kamae* (single-leg) pose.

Hicho no kamae represents the attitude that protects the freedom of the *ohzora ni mau tamashi*, or "sky-dancing spirits."

The right leg pushes up from the earth as the left leg sends out a kick. In this position you flow and play in the *yugen* realm of the netherworld.

Always allow both legs to play in *kukan*, or "space."

Masaaki Hatsumi assumes the *hicho no kamae* while Stephen Hayes takes the defensive *ichimonji no kamae*. *Kamae* is the body's way of expressing what is held in the heart.

Masaaki Hatsumi again takes the *hicho no kamae*, to express his tactic of flying away from the fight. Stephen Hayes assumes the *jumonji no kamae* this time. Also referred to as *inori no kamae*, or "posture of the pledge," vowing to do his best to ward off unnecessary conflict.

The belt-tying method for sword work is very different from that normally used with the martial arts training suit. Allow the gap of space between the two loops of the belt to better secure the sword scabbard to your body. This way, the scabbard will feel like a part of your body, and will not accidentally swing away, out of control.

Stephen Hayes assumes the *daijodan no kamae* while Masaaki Hatsumi stares at the attacker's brow from a crouching position. This way, Hatsumi can be aware of his attacker's total body in motion.

When the attacker cuts down with his sword, the defender angles back and away while grabbing the moving sword with his *shuko*-wielding right hand.

Masaaki Hatsumi's two *shuko* twist the sword out of the attacker's grip.

Securing the sword with his left *shuko*, Hatsumi uses his right *shuko* to attack Hayes's face.

Masaaki Hatsumi then sweeps down with his right *shuko* and rocks back to pull the sword away from the attacker. The attacker naturally wants to chase after his sword, bending forward to retrieve the moving weapon.

The defender then lifts the sword with a *sanshin gyaku hangetsu* swing, and pierces down at the staggering attacker.

Stephen Hayes approaches from the *gyaku seigan no kamae* (reverse eye-aim posture), while Masaaki Hatsumi watches him from the natural *shuko kasumi no kamae*, or "hand-claw-hazing posture."

The attacker lunges forward with a piercing stab. Defender Hatsumi moves only the slightest distance to allow the blade to miss him, while running his right *shuko* along the moving blade.

Masaaki Hatsumi attacks Stephen Hayes's left hand with his right *shuko*. When Hayes lifts his left hand to avoid damage, Hatsumi responds by gripping the attacker's right thumb with the claws of his right *shuko*.

The defender's left *shuko* secures the sword tip from the back, deriving its power from the defender's body in motion. Hatsumi lifts up with his right *shuko* to spin the attacker.

The sword seems to disappear only to reappear again with a stab to the torso.

Masaaki Hatsumi's left *shuko* secures the blade as he steps forward to execute the cut.

With a single pull on the sword, the attacker ends up on his back, on his way to a place "among the Buddhas."

When using the *shuko* in combat, it is not necessary to use big aggressive actions. Even the slightest twist of the claw into its target will move the most powerful of fighters.

Shuko kumite, "Bringing the hands together."

The attacker punches with his right hand. With a subtle body shift, defender Hatsumi reaches out with both *shuko* to cover both of Hayes's fists at the same moment.

Hatsumi pushes Hayes's left arm with his right *shuko*, automatically forcing Hayes's right arm to extend.

Masaaki Hatsumi uses his right knee to apply
leverage against the attacker's left knee and
forces him down gently in a smooth flow.

The defender's left leg pins the attacker's left
arm, while his left *shuko* hooks and pulls up on
his right arm. The right *shuko* pins the attacker's left leg.

Even as the enemy approaches, a true human being will give him one more chance to smile and shake hands.

Peaceful intentions were not enough, the attacker grabs the defender in an attempt to throw him, but Masaaki Hatsumi allows his body to turn with the attack to prevent the throw.

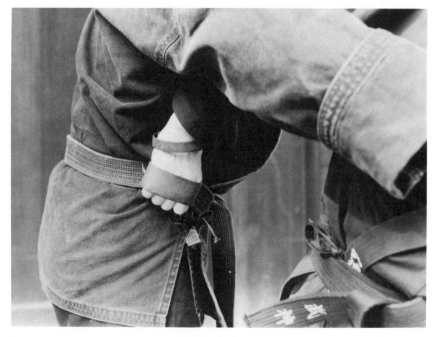

If the attacker still wants to continue, Hatsumi can grab the torso with his right *shuko*.

Stephen Hayes recoils in surprise, releasing his grip.

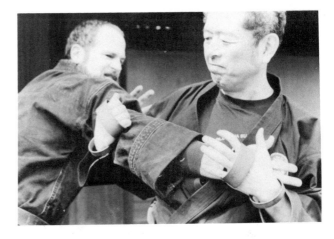

If the attack continues, defender Hatsumi can hug the attacker's arm to his body, applying gentle pressure with the claws of his two *shuko*.

Hatsumi then pivots to his own right, ending up under the attacker's barred right arm. He is then in a position to complete a *ganseki nage* (forward throw).

5

NATURAL LIVING AND MARTIAL FRIENDS

We sit in the front room of Masaaki Hatsumi's home, huddled around a glowing kerosene stove. We are surrounded by towering canyon walls of dusty books, vining plants, paintings and photo panels, and the bone-aligning clinic equipment used by the ninja doctor to assist his patients back to health. A few timidly silent birds crouch in cages suspended close to the ceiling, safely far above the reach of the dozens of cats that share the dwelling with Masaaki and Mariko Hatsumi. Our knees press up against a small wobbly table constructed from a crosscut tree trunk, and the ever-ubiquitous cups of pale green Japanese tea sit steaming before us.

The grandmaster is busy grinding an ink stick against the flat lower surface of the small black stone basin. He dips the end of the stick in the pool of water and grinds away with rhythmic pushes from his wrist and shoulder. Slowly, in degrees so subtle that it is difficult to register the changes as they take place, the small pool of water darkens and becomes the *sumi* ink that Masaaki Hatsumi will use to brush the Japanese kanji characters on the fresh white paper scroll that waits unrolled in the next room. He talks as he works, ever the cordial host, ever the teacher, ever the artist.

Holding the black stone ink basin in his left hand and the huge bulging pointed brush in his right, the grandmaster moves from the conversation pit across the room to a space on the floor that has been specially cleared for this work of calligraphy. The heels of his slippers, standard in-house footwear in this country where all shoes are left by the entryway door, slap against the worn wooden floorboards as he moves with a brisk shuffling gait. Rumiko and I follow him to the scroll, ducking and weaving as necessary to negotiate our way through the crowded museum structure that is home to Masaaki Hatsumi. Looking at all the familiar paintings, cabinets, and pieces of furniture that nudge corners against one another and give a sort of foundation to the clutter in this room, it is like being among old silent friends once again. Listening to the ticking of the stove fire, tasting the steam from the huge dented kettle atop the heater, I find myself pleasantly filled with nostalgia, as I always am when here, for those days so long behind me.

Dr. Hatsumi crouches over the scroll, his ink-saturated brush poised in hand. He is staring at the brilliant whiteness of the paper, eyes intently peering downward, as though he has forgotten just what it was that he had intended to write. He has not, of course, forgotten, and he is suddenly moved by the spirit for which he has been waiting. The black-pointed tip of the brush dives for the waiting expanse of white below it, like the honed tip of a *shuriken* intent on piercing its target. In an explosion of strokes, swirls, and stabs, the brush dances and lurches its way down the wide strip of paper. The white is now eternally host to the black, as the Japanese-brushed characters soak into the weave of the paper in permanent and timeless lodging.

The nine syllables of Toshitsugu Takamatsu's secret *kuji* mantra appear before the three of us in graphic boldness. The eternal power of this phrase was forged through the three-fold melding of illusion-piercing strategy, unwavering intention, and committed action almost a millenium ago. Roared from the throat in eye-to-eye battle, and baptized under the flow of the resolute tears of conviction, this mantric oath symbolizing the grasping of the inevitable had vibrated on the lips, behind the eyes, and in the hearts of the warriors of our lineage for centuries. As the brush is lifted in final pause, page filled and ink spent, the power of this *kuji* is handed on to me, to be cherished and further empowered by my own family through the generations that will unfold into the future a half a world away from this silent wooden room.

I marvel out loud at the power of the mind in transforming the mundane into magic. Ultimately, it is one's own self-created belief that determines that which is inspiring and that which is ignored. These nine syllables on this unfurled scroll could either be things of power or things of confusion, based solely on the perceiver's personal background. The seasoned warrior, having been through enough of the tempering process of a lifetime, could take this *kuji* string of sounds and images, fully realizing its source in creation, and embody it daily as a means of further extending the capacity of his own personal power. The uninitiated, peering out at life from the limitations of a tunnel of inexperience, would not even see these brushed and chanted characters as having anything to do with the martial arts at all.

Slowly, my mind acknowledges a third possible direction for application of the lore of the ninja's *kuji no ho* teachings. There is positive engagement of the power of intention. There is also neutral ignorance of the entire concept itself. In addition to positive and neutral, there is that third, and highly negative, application as well. Hesitantly, as though the mere thought itself had the dark power to corrupt, I acknowledge mentally how easy it would be to deceive all the naive and unsophisticated hopefuls that are drawn to the enticing promises of power inherent in all I teach as the art of the ninja invisible warriors. I know fully well that there are many who would so willingly give anything asked of them for the powers of *kuji* magic without having first to go through the extremely risky process of personal power cultivation along the warrior path to enlightenment.

I have seen some characters take a little knowledge of spiritual talk and transform it into a highly successful con game in which the world is duped into seeing them as wizards or masters. It happens in the religious world, the financial world, the health world, and the martial arts world as well. I look down at the wet and glistening Japanese characters before me and look up again at Masaaki Hatsumi. There are people out there publishing books on *kuji* methods, I comment to my teacher. He laughs out loud happily and shakes his head. Using highly poetic language, he cheerfully makes a barely decipherable comment on how false magic is a sure path to one's own destruction.

Immediately, the night seems somehow a little chillier, a little darker, even in the warmth and light of this room.

RH: Unfortunately, several of our students are under the impression that some of the things you do, such as *kukinage* (throwing an attacker without touching any part of his body), are magic or wizardry. You say that the reason you can do *kukinage*-type techniques is because you have a long history of going through hard fundamental combat training. It is not something that you can learn to do instantly, is it? I like to believe that.

MH: Yes, yes. Exactly. That's it. There's no magic. In fact, if the timing just happens to be right, even a novice may be able to pull off something like throwing another person without touching him.

RH: Some students do not want to hear that the reason why Dr. Hatsumi can do things like *kukinage* is that he has a long history of realistic martial arts training. We tell them it is not magic. You have to engage in a long period of training to be able to do things like that consistently. But some students don't want to hear that. It sounds too much like work. They want to have it overnight, instantly.

SKH: Actually, we have lost several students in the past due to this desire for "magical mystery training." I know that these gullible persons were conned into believing that some clever tricks were indeed magic or wizardry, but those people do not want to hear that from me. I guess I spoiled their fantasy.

MH: Human beings are easily trapped by the tricks of these devils. Some people have in their inborn nature a need to gain attention or admiration by deceiving or tricking other people through falsely represented techniques or powers. They are like devils operating that way, leading innocent people away from truth. Their abilities to do these tricks are not based on extensive training efforts to cultivate legitimate skills.

SKH: To me, conning believing students seems to be a sure way to accumulate a hopeless mass of sticky karmic debts. If you believe in karmic processes, that is.

MH: These scoundrels have this kind of nature by birth. If they can use it in a noble direction, then it will be of benefit to them in the real world of combat.

SKH: Deception can be a ninja tactic when used to promote self-protection. What I object to is this deception used to boost one's ego by attracting crowds of naive followers. It seems immoral to me.

MH: Human beings love to be impressed or awed by the mysterious and unknown. We would all like to have an unearthly "close encounter." But in a way, to be impressed is to create the natural base for self-defense.

SKH: We notice that something is out of the ordinary and we mentally move to do what is necessary to integrate it in our world.

MH: Of course it is also true that when you are impressed, you can easily become a willing victim and fall into the trap of the trickster's technique. You can interpret it that way, too.

RH: To those people who were involved with our training before and are now attracted to these phony mystery men, ninjutsu was just an elaborate fantasy. As they practiced ninjutsu with Stephen, it turned out not to be a fantasy. They realized that mastery takes a lot of work. Then they wandered off in search of another fantasy.

SKH: These are not bad people we are talking about here. They are just naive. They are in search of entertainment rather than education, although they themselves would of course argue this point. I am not offended by their going off after these fantasies. I guess I am just a little disappointed in how easily, how willingly, they were conned. Perhaps *my* fantasy is that the world is more intelligent and discriminating than it really is!

MH: True, true. Therefore, I feel it is important to bring out a book like this. If I tell the truth, people will be forced to hear it. That is why we are talking so candidly here today. This might only be a small volume, but it will be an important one.

SKH: It is hard to compete with fantasy. Reality pales beside what I call the "Dungeons and Dragons" mentality. That's a fantasy game played by young people in America. Too many times, the fantasy of the toy drifts over into real life and the players come to believe that they really *are* the characters in the game. I suppose it is a symptom of not having a stimulating enough life.

MH: You have been approaching the martial arts with a very sincere heart, Hayes-san. As I always remind you, it could be said that you may even have too sincere a heart. Anyway, now some people are trying to argue with what you teach and are hoping that they can trip you up. Well, this is a highly important time. I can tell, because my sixth sense is very keen. I hope this book will be published as a literal translation of my thoughts, word by word.

SKH: Well, maybe I am too sincere. I have an acting background and I have a good imagination, so I know I could do a great job conning people into believing that I was some kind of wizard if I wanted to. I could play the role and live the comic

You have to go all the way, be totally immersed in order to know the full truth or power of a thing. It is just like the drunk's experience of being delightfully intoxicated. There is something so pleasant, so thoroughly wonderful in a complete and fully total experience of a thing.

book, stereotypical ninja life, giving the impression of being half Rambo and half Obiwan Kenobi. I could get rid of my children, get rid of my material possessions, live in the woods and live an all-natural life, but I already know that is an extreme form of weakness.

To tell the truth, I have to admit that I would not want to be surrounded by the kind of people that could be conned that easily. I can't believe how easily these grown adults fell for these illusions. It's creepy really, the willingness of some people to be deceived. I'm looking for strong souls, powerful people with whom to share my time. (Laughing.) Perhaps the ninja boom is not too much longer lived with that kind of attitude on my part. Most folks seemed bored with my insistence on realistic demonstrable power in life.

MH: You know, I do not care whether or not the so-called ninja boom disappears. I just want to speak out on truth. You see, what is ultimately true will never disappear. Those people who came to me and trained with me for a long time really understand the truth embodied by this art. The beginners, the novices, they can have no way of understanding.

SKH: It's something you have to be there to experience. I read some of these silly claims made by these made-up ninja masters who appeared in the press after the ninja boom got rolling, and I laugh out loud at their claims. There is no way these claims could be true, and yet customers willingly suspend rational judgement and give them money for "ninja training." I understand why their claims are impossible, because I've been there, but the rest of the world has no idea of why I can say what I say. They have no way of understanding how I understand what I understand. They

haven't been there and I have. That's all I can say. Only one who has been there can know the ring of truth as opposed to the thud of falsehood.

MH: Here's a funny analogy. To those who have not had the experience of drinking *sake*, no matter how hard you try to explain to them how good it is, they still have no idea what you are talking about. Only those who can let loose and get themselves drunk know the charm of *sake*. You have to go all the way, be totally immersed in order to know the full truth or power of a thing. It is just like the drunk's experience of being delightfully intoxicated. There is something so pleasant, so thoroughly wonderful in a complete and fully total experience of a thing. It is not devilish fantasy.

RH: This idea of an all-natural lifestyle away from society is another popular ideal. Some people want to believe that is what they have to do to be a real warrior or ninja.

MH: I talk of living naturally, too, but I am also very much in touch with reality. I act appropriately in accordance with the times in which we live. Certainly, it is important to understand nature, but I also see the importance of being able to operate in the everyday reality of the modern world as well. The balance between "living naturally" and being realistic is crucial.

There are some people who like to brag about living a totally natural life, only eating natural foods and wearing natural clothing fibers. Now in Japan, for example, there is a growing portion of the population that chooses to eat *genmai* unpolished rice instead of the more popular *hakumai* polished rice. There is now a demand for organically grown vegetables, and an aversion to meats and so on. Fans of this sort of diet say that their way of living is the best, but to me, this sounds like something that a weakling would say. From my point of view, if you cannot exist and do well on whatever is at hand, then you have a weak body.

SKH: They have cultivated a new weakness by insisting that things can only be one way for themselves to be satisfied.

MH: We are now living in an age that requires endurance, adaptability, and stamina. Look at the insects. We spray over and over again to try to kill them, but the insects never die out. The spray might slow them down for a while, but there are always some who survive. The power of life is strong, but human beings are weakening their own power of life by talking of such things as hiding from all pollutants. They will not let their bodies get used to what is happening in the world we share.

To let your body get used to the nature of the particular time and place in which you live is in a way the nature of being realistic. A lot of people forget to think and live realistically. They believe something magical will happen if they go off to the mountains and train there. But to live in the real world is much more difficult than to live surrounded by nature. To me, a naturalist is one who leads a leisurely life. That is not being a warrior. That is simply a man on vacation. I say things like this very severely or caustically. The manner in which the early-American Indians lived is wonderful, being so close to nature, but we also have to acknowledge the cold hard fact that the Indians no longer flourish in today's world. They did not make it. It is also true that anything that lasts only a short time, a magic trick or an illusion, can be clarified, can have its trick or secret discovered by others.

SKH: The baffled audience can suddenly catch on and see through the trick.

MH: Those who are immature will be attracted to such tricks.

As long as they are happy, I suppose it is fine, as long as it does not go too far and turn into some kind of dangerous self-destructive cult. But as those people grow older, they will come to see the tricks behind the magic act.

RH: The ones that we call the victims of the tricksters, the ones who left, are all young people.

MH: They will be back soon, if they are really seeking the timeless secrets. It is like a first love. I have gone through a lot of first loves, so I know the feeling. I fell in love, got my heart broken, fell in love, got my heart broken, a seemingly endless cycle. Finally I found the real thing, and that is the one I married. The same thing can be said about the martial arts. Because of peoples' ignorance and fascination for the unfamiliar, a boom can be created. If it is all known and familiar, there will be no boom. Because ninjutsu is an unknown art, the fantasy is created. Since it is not known, people anxiously look to it in hope.

As you know, there is always a little fantasy in every reality. The fantastic can indeed be found in what is real and authentic, if you are willing to look for it through adult eyes. It is just that the truly fantastic shows up in a different kind of manifestation than that which is sought out by the immature. The real thing will fulfill the dreams of mature persons. Of course I am not talking about age in years here when I speak of mature and immature. I am talking about depth of experience and awareness of the significance of that experience. I think this is what is needed most in America. There will be no real growth as a human being no matter how many years of life you happen to collect if you are not aware.

RH: Stephen went through times when people talked badly about him. Students that he had taught for years suddenly turned on him and pretended that they did not really get all they got from him. Bud Malmstrom had the same experience, people turned on his dojo, and you had the same thing happen to you. Those people, instead of realizing their own faults, thrive on criticizing others. It is a weakness of human beings . . .

MH: No. It is a dirtiness of human beings.

SKH: Sure, I have been on the receiving end of this weakness, this dirtiness as you call it. And of course it always comes from behind my back. For some reason, the wisecracks and slurs all come through the rumor grapevine or through the printed media, and never in my presence where the critic would have to deal with me face to face.

MH: Well then, let's sympathize with each other. I know exactly what you are talking about. As I said before, as you become more and more recognized, you will generate more and more criticism. Nichiren was stoned by jealous people who refused to understand him. Even a holy one like Jesus the Christ was treated the same way. A holy person like Christ was misunderstood and forced to drag his own cross through the streets on his back. We are not anywhere near the level of a Christ, so how could we escape the cruel labors thrust upon us? If even the holy are abused, then who are we to expect to be well-treated by those we could serve?

But that is fine, isn't it? I think that is important to acknowledge. That is why I want to talk at this point. You have trained and struggled and endured enough to receive these teachings. You went through plenty of hardships. I am happy that my son has grown up and I am happy that we can talk together on this level. I want you to think of this petty jealousy and criticism behind your back as a minor thing, a tiny meaningless spot in your life. I want you to think of those things as fertilizer for your growth.

Those criticisms, those hardships, are presented to you as a test to see whether you will become greater. If you take it in that light, such things will not make you unhappy or angry. In zen training, it is said that enlightenment is always right there under your feet. You just have to recognize it for what it is. I know that you underwent a lot of hardship. I made you go through those trials and agonies for a purpose. Since you overcame those hardships, you are here.

You have become the holy warrior hero from your novel *Tulku*. Therefore, great men like the Dalai Lama are willing to spend time with you personally. Indeed, Hayes-san, this is the result of your efforts and your personal character. Because you are an evolved person, he was willing to meet with you. It is not easy to gain access to great and accomplished persons. That's why I enjoy talking with you. (Laughing.) Maybe we are both holy warrior heroes. We can be proud of that.

SKH: I will agree, but with a laugh in my voice. It is true that if I don't believe in myself, no one else will. But I do not want people holding the impression that I take myself too seriously, that I am posing as some great leader.

MH: Certainly. I know who I am, and at the same time, I do not want to make slaves of my students. I want them to be free. Therefore, I award ranks up to second or third degree according

I do not like to be referred to as a teacher. I do not want to be seen as way above everyone else. I want to have friends. Then we can talk. We are free to discuss anything.

to the students' present level of fighting ability. Do you understand this? It's not for the purpose of making them fight each other. After handling the formality of a rank license, what they have as their personal qualities becomes more important. In all, our martial art is something that you have to grasp on your own. That is the essence of our training. It is not salvation by blind faith.

It is not a matter of who is wrong or right. So conversely, I am thankful because I had detractors in my life. There were people who badmouthed me, but I chose to consider their criticism as a form of praising my greatness. I am confident in myself in the role of *soke*. Don't you think so? Takamatsu-sensei gave me the title of *soke*. If I do not have confidence in my ability to fill that role, then I owe my apologies to him. You are the one who is the closest to me right now, Hayes-san. That's why I feel comfortable speaking this way with you.

Hardship is important. It is heaven sent. For example, you gave birth to two children, Rumiko. You suffered, it was hard wasn't it? But that is why you are a mother that your children respect. To be respected, you have to endure going through the tempering of hardship. Don't you agree?

Life is the same. Heaven has given you these lessons. So for a man to become a top figure, it is a matter of course that he will have to suffer hardship. Look at me now. I have so many students, and you have many students. We both are prolific. Therefore, we are bound to go through this same ordeal over and over again. It's like the agony a mother goes through giving birth again and again.

It's easy to wonder why I have had to suffer like this. I can find myself thinking that perhaps I am doing something wrong. But then I refuse to acknowledge those doubts, and I continue to reaffirm my own rightness. Now I want to share my experience of these hardships with you.

This is what I mean by the concept of *buyu*, or "martial friends." It is quite different from the usual teacher-student relationship. That is why I do not like to be referred to as a teacher. I do not want to be seen as way above everyone else. I want to have friends. Then we can talk. We are free to discuss anything. So even though this volume may be a thin one, I want everything that I say here to be in there.

RH: There are a lot of people who do not seem to be able to reach the core essence of the martial arts.

MH: Before you investigate that matter, it is important to note the fact that the modern martial arts that have the most public recognition, such as judo, karate, aikido, kendo, and so forth, were born during the time of the Meiji era (1868–1912). The Edo period (1603–1867) was a long and peaceful time. I wonder, in that era of over two-and-a-half centuries of peaceful isolation, how many real fighting arts were kept alive.

Before the Edo period, in the late 1500s, guns were introduced. The introduction of firearms to Japan determined the outcome of the history-making struggles leading to a new set of rulers for Japan. So even at the beginning of the Edo period almost four centuries ago, instead of sword or spear or hand-to-hand fighting, the gun had become the principal weapon of warfare in Japan. Traditional Japanese martial arts were changed unalterably at that point.

Historical martial arts scrolls were written from the end of the Muromachi period (1392–1573), Takamatsu-sensei told me. Unless it was a peaceful era, people did not have the free time to sit down and write on a scroll what they had been taught. So perhaps those scrolls that were written during peaceful times were swallowed blindly as being the ultimate in true martial techniques.

SKH: Even though the writer may never have used the techniques he described in actual combat.

MH: Scrolls, or *densho*, can have meanings at many levels. A famous academic researcher named Inazo Nitobe said in his book that the true area of study lies between the printed words. *Kukan*, the space between the words, is important. Those who know this will be the true scholars. The same thing can be said about the *makimono* scrolls as total units. There is a significant gap of space between one scroll and the next. There may only be one word written as a clue to some grander truth. It is not the transmission of *kata* or technique. In one word there can be infinite movements contained.

SKH: It seems that the Japanese student is culturally familiar with philosophical concepts such as the *godai* (the five elements) or the *tenchijin* (three-level energy manifestation), whereas a foreign person who comes into contact with these things is lost. He has to ask specifically, "What do you mean by this 'earth, water, fire,' and so on?" Because the cultural parts of the training, the parts that a Japanese person picks up naturally as a part of growing up in Japan, seem so foreign and complicated, a lot of foreigners can become discouraged and give up before they have a chance to get the true essence of the art.

MH: Let me show you. You write from bottom to top—earth, water, fire, wind, and void. So as you can see, in nature there is the ground below and the sky above.

SKH: So that is *ten* as heaven overhead and *chi* as earth under foot.

MH: Water comes from above. Fire is warmth, like the sun. Wind moves prompted by heat. Then there is the sky, *sora* or *ku*. The Japanese written character can also be translated as "void."

SKH: That is a translation that most westerners really get tripped up over. It seems very foreign to the Western realm of philosophical thought. I think "void" is a bad translation. To us, void means "not valid" or "nothing there," and *ku* is not really nothing there. I like "formless potential" or "devoid of specific attributes," myself.

MH: When you analyze this written character for *ku*, or void, from the point of view of mikkyo symbolism, you find that it is made up of brush strokes meaning "hole" and "root." The hole symbolizes the female sexual organ, and the root symbolizes the male organ. Therefore, I feel that *ku* represents the force of things uniting in potential. I think you can interpret it as "heaven." Or you could interpret it as hell, because there is always *kyojitsu*, the appearance of truth as falsehood and falsehood as truth. From earth, the progression leads on up the hierarchy to the void, a total of five steps.

I think this book is an important way to let people know that there is a way of interpreting these things the way I do. There may be many ways of interpreting these five elemental manifestations from the Buddhist point of view. You know, a characteristic aspect of the oriental way of approaching things is to make them complicated, therefore creating more mystery around a thing. I am not necessarily saying this is good or bad. It's just that it takes so much time and effort to be able to work your way through to

Mystery is not necessarily magic. It is very human, and historic. Mysterious workings are a part of the real world. This is important. We are not talking about comic book entertainment here.

an understanding of the essential concept if you are approaching it religiously or philosophically.

Well, I interpret this *godai* concept in a simple manner. The *gorin no to* (five-levelled tower) has one element written on each portion. So I think that it is necessary to interpret oriental philosophy in simple terms so that all people can understand.

SKH: The simplicity of these symbols is their beauty, if Western students could just get through the cultural barriers to realize that this is not mumbo-jumbo metaphysics. The mystical does not have to be mysterious. This is down-to-earth common sense. (Laughing.) Oops! There goes the fantasy. There go the students.

MH: At another level of symbolism, our five fingers represent the five elements—*chi, sui, ka, fu, ku,* from little finger up to thumb. Some people insist that using these energy channeling rings is a form of auto-suggestion, or self-intoxication if we refer to it in a negative light. Others refer to it as a form of spiritual unification. If some people have been practicing this sort of thing for an extended period, they may be able to bring about some sort of miraculous phenomena, or tune in to things happening at other levels of the world. This is what Takamatsu-sensei taught me.

RH: Again, you emphasize training for mastery. It is not an instant trick.

MH: Here's an example. Remember when you accidentally cut your finger open in the kitchen when I was staying at your home in Ohio, Rumiko? It did not hurt. I did not say anything, no chants or mantras. I just did this (making a series of cutting motions in the air), and your finger never bothered you. It is said that when Kobo Daishi [monk Kukai (774–835), founder of the Shingon sect of esoteric Buddhism] merely put his hand over a sick person, they were relieved.

Human beings can seem to have mysterious power. I think when you were injured, Rumiko, I wanted you to get better so badly that my intention took a form of its own. So perhaps my desire for you to get better was so strong that it reached divine forces, and prompted what we might call instant healing. There was no pain.

In truth, it must also be acknowledged that those who do not train, those who do not constantly strive to perform to their utmost, those who do not believe, or those who are not in tune with what I am doing, are unable to be affected by me. I cannot take their pain away or assist with their healing process. I think it is necessary as an honest and sincere person to realize that sometimes these things happen and sometimes they do not. You are not almighty. If you acknowledge this truth, then you are more likely to avoid falling into the trap of becoming a dishonest con artist.

There have been a lot of mysterious cases that have happened around me. For example, I avoided your unseen punch from behind, Hayes-san. That could be considered as one of those mysterious incidents. Many other things have happened. That leads us to the real *jumon* and *ketsu-in*. These symbols of vow and finger entwining even appear in a picture of Amaterasu Omikami that I was given.

Takamatsu-sensei used to tell me that it is a fortunate thing that I am in connection with some divine force in the universe. I accept this mystery for what it is. I believe that such things can and do exist in the world of human beings. If such connections are used wrongly, or are taken in the wrong direction, they can become destructive things. Such abuse would be a form of heresy. Hold onto your pure and straightforward heart, Takamatsu-sensei used to tell me. To obtain such a heart, the basic requirement is *ninpo taijutsu* training. From there, you go on to enlightenment.

RH: This is a follow up to the previous question. In studying Japanese martial arts, there are philosophical backgrounds, religious backgrounds. Do foreign students have to study these backgrounds if they want to learn the authentic Japanese martial arts? Or are you saying that in ninjutsu these things will be naturally understood as you practice taijutsu?

MH: You can come to an understanding of all the various levels of meaning in this art, provided that you study under a good instructor. This is the only thing I want to say. For example, Hayes-san, you have been practicing this art for many years. You understand me. That means you understand and are connected with a part of the *shinkai*, the realm of divine consciousness.

Once again, the fact that you were able to meet with the Dalai Lama deserves acknowledgment, because he is far too busy and important to see just anyone. You were born under that kind of star, Hayes-san. To be able to spend time with a great soul like the Dalai Lama, you must have something that connects you to him, some mysterious linkage at some level. You are the one who caused the spark that set the ninja boom on fire. Everyone knows that. Now, you may be moving on to something more, something beyond the ninja boom. I feel that you were born under some kind of special star. In a way, this is something wonderfully mysterious.

Mystery is not necessarily magic. It is very human, and historic. Mysterious workings are a part of the real world. This is important. We are not talking about comic book entertainment here. To be connected with splendid religious training, with splendid philosophical training, means blending together simultaneously with the highest universal sense. You know me well enough to know I'm not bragging, so I can say to you straightforwardly that I somehow seem to be in contact with that higher strata.

That's why I always said that I was a UFO. Maybe that's how I can reach those higher cosmic levels. Here's that same old UFO joke again, huh? But even though I first made up that UFO comment as a joke, the humor in the original comical label could be transformed into a sober statement like this.

Small things always have the potential of bringing on major significances. For example, the act of simple-mindedly playing around with a single tiny match could result in a horrendously big fire that could destroy an entire city.

Does any of this make sense? Can you understand the point of all this? Well, you may not fully understand, but there is something that you might feel as having touched you or gotten through, isn't there? That is the essence of learning taijutsu. You just cannot figure out my taijutsu. But there is something there that gets through to you when you train with me, right? You somehow get the point of the given action I might spring on you in the dojo. Attaining enlightenment is the same process. It doesn't do any good to work at trying to figure it out intellectually. Something splendid lies at that point of being reached. That is what leads you to enlightenment. Being touched is one form of the enlightenment experience.

However, you must beware of being touched or moved by something negative. I am referring back to what we were discussing previously, about immature and open-hearted young people being "touched" by manipulative con artists. They want so badly to believe in what they want, that they do not realize they are being lead dangerously astray from the true warrior ideal they claim to have pledged themselves to in the first place.

The *bisento* (battlefield) long-handled broad-sword is a very heavy weapon. It is essential to use the entire body motion to swing and drop the blade, or the extreme weight of the weapon will quickly rob the user of his strength. The *bisento* is capable of crushing through armor, cutting through a horse's neck, and subdueing all evil that comes against it.

Stephen Hayes maintains the sword *chudan no kamae*, while Masaaki Hatsumi takes his position in the *seigan no kamae* posture.

Hayes attacks with a right-to-left diagonal cut to move Hatsumi's weapon out of his way. Hatsumi retreats with his right leg to avoid the sword strike entirely, supporting the weight of the *bisento* handle on his left thigh.

Masaaki Hatsumi advances with his right leg and arm to cut into the attacker's sword handle with the *bisento* blade. Note carefully that Dr. Hatsumi's right leg (rather than either of his arms) does all the work.

Defender Hatsumi leans his body forward slightly, cutting into the upper portion of the attacker's left arm.

With a simple pull from his left leg, Hatsumi sends the pointed tip of the *bisento* blade up into Hayes's throat.

Defender Hatsumi then rolls the handle to realign the blade and lets it plummet downward like a waterfall.

Stephen Hayes positions himself in a right *hasso no kamae* across from Masaaki Hatsumi's low *gedan no kamae*. Hatsumi drops the heavy blade toward Hayes's left foot as he moves forward with a crouching cross step.

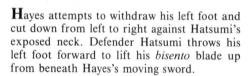
Hayes attempts to withdraw his left foot and cut down from left to right against Hatsumi's exposed neck. Defender Hatsumi throws his left foot forward to lift his *bisento* blade up from beneath Hayes's moving sword.

Defender Hatsumi steps in with his right foot to interrupt and overpower the attacker's sword cut.

The defender then rolls the *bisento* handle in his hands to change the angle of his blade. He allows the weapon's weight to drop the back of the blade onto the back of his attacker's neck. In all actions with the ninja's *bisento*, the weapon's weight is used as an advantage.

Once again, a rolling action changes the angle of the blade, and the falling weight of the weapon provides the cutting power.

Masaaki Hatsumi pulls his right leg back to effect a finishing cut to the back of his downed attacker's neck.

In *jigoku gyaku otoshi,* the attacker advances with a savage and reckless heart. At the moment his feverish energies are expended, the ninja's spirit escorts him further on, into the valley of hell.

In this technique, referred to as *sannin dori yoko guruma,* three attackers surround Masaaki Hatsumi and bind both his wrists and his neck. He relaxes all body tension and avoids resisting the attackers.

By using multiple actions from the bones and joints of the body, he drifts sideways to break the balance of his three struggling adversaries.

When the first one loses his balance, the remaining two attackers are immediately pitted against one another in surprise, rendering their centers of balance unstable.

The attackers do not fall as a result of Masaaki Hatsumi's power or strength. They topple as a result of their conflicting and now misdirected tension.

All three hit the ground unsure of just why it was that they were unable to hold on to the non-resisting victim.

Sannin dori tatsumaki, or "three-man tornado escape," uses twisting power to topple the three adversaries. First, the defender concentrates on using the power of his attacker's rear neck choke.

He folds forward and disturbs the rear attacker's stability and balance.

At that point, defender Hatsumi rolls sideways like a snake.

Dr. Hatsumi uses his body as a fulcrum to drop his attackers.

The adversaries tumble over and into one another.

Defender Hatsumi uses his head, right foot, and left knee to attack and immobilize his three downed adversaries.

6
THE FUTURE OF NINJUTSU

The three of us move out into the silent darkened street. In a tumble of quiet activity, we slip into shoes, move the dogs through the doorway without tangling the leashes too hopelessly, and turn back to slide the glass-and-wood door panel closed on its screechy metal tracks. The three dogs lurch and pull at their tethers, anxious to be up and outside once again. The claws on their feet scratch and click against the cool bricks of the narrow street that stretches out in front of Masaaki Hatsumi's home and clinic, and we have to move briskly to keep up with the anxious animals. It is well after midnight, and no one else stirs in this sleepy little section of central Noda City.

We had gone into the back of the grandmaster's home to get the dogs. The three animals had been asleep on mats stretched out beneath a collection of miniature shrine structures built right up next to the low ceiling. That small room had been our dojo in the days of the 1970s that had first brought me to Japan in search of the timeless teachings of power which had been handed down for centuries by the last inheritors of the *shinobi* legacy. Now filled with crates of antiques, boxes of historical weapons, and a series of mats, cages, and cushions that constituted the sleeping quarters

of a collection of cats, birds, and dogs, the little room was still
reverently maintained as Dr. Hatsumi's central shrine to the
spiritual ancestors of our nine martial ryu traditions.

The little wooden shrines were wreathed in clipped *sakaki*
greens stuffed into a collection of brass vases. Odd numbers—
fives, sevens, and nines—of white candles in brass holders fronted
each shrine, and seemingly countless pairs of miniature lanterns
glowed beside and behind the structures. The main *kamidana*
shelf held a small gilded statue of Toshitsugu Takamatsu in seated
folded-leg posture. Dr. Hatsumi had carved the likeness of his
departed teacher. He had a practice of using that miniature
golden likeness on its suspended shelf to bless or charge his
manuscripts, special presents, or archival works by placing them
on the shelf for set numbers of days and nights. I found my
teacher's quiet and yet consistent devotion to his own teacher,
now long since entombed, to be quite moving and inspiring.

We walk along the cobbles of this street of shuttered shops in
darkened Noda City. The air is cool, fresh, and bracing, and is
permeated with but a hint of the tangy soy sauce aroma that
characterizes the primary identity of this centuries-old Chiba
Prefecture town. The dogs are an explosion of joy upon being
released into the night air. Kagemaru, a small high-strung black
male surges forward in the lead. London, a mangey little mongrel,
and Madoka, the lumbering Afghan hound, lope along in pursuit.
The dogs race against their leashes after hours of captivity. One
by one, they finally pause with great urgency to relieve themselves
in huge running puddles that glisten in the moonlight.

I think of my country home in America, and the acres of wooded terrain through which in complete freedom run our Akita hunting dogs. Those husky animals half a world away could have no way of knowing of the lives that these beasts live, restricted to their small quarters save for these walks three times a day. I muse in silent respect over all that life has presented me that I myself take for granted as well.

The home and clinic of Masaaki and Mariko Hatsumi stands out in stark contrast from the rest of the buildings on the narrow street. Where others gleam as modern and sleek rebuilt structures, sharing nothing at all in common with their former selves save the very location on which they stand, the Hatsumi family building is the last of the post-war antiques, a structure of weathered wood, dusty frosted glass, rusting corrugated steel panels, and long-faded paint flaking away from untold years before. The front of their homey dwelling is a depth of potted and crated plants, shrubs, and miniature trees, whereas the other buildings boast only concrete steps and steel railings.

Ironically, in spite of the truth of just who it is that lives in the building, the faded sign over the door mentions only the Hatsumi Seikotsu Clinic. Nowhere on the building is there a reference to the martial tradition based behind those nondescript walls so easy to miss on this quiet side street in a little town on the banks of the Edo River.

Rumiko, the grandmaster, and I walk along through the night streets, deep in our continuing conversation. We pass by familiar landmarks that had long ago become a part of the eclectic collection of sights and sites, experiences and images, people and peoples, that contributed to make up the weave of the rich fabric of the days and years of my life.

Here is the bench at the bus stop in front of the Kikkoman offices where I used to sit and wait for transportation every Wednesday and Saturday night after training in the home of the grandmaster of ninjutsu. There is the little workman's clothing shop, now barricaded shut with midnight's locks and shutters, where I bought my first pair of tabi, all those years before every American martial art magazine was filled with order blanks for the fad-inspired black canvas "ninja shoes." Here we are once again on the grounds of Atago Jinja, the huge dark shrine looming up, all carved shadows in the moonlight. We pass by several of the shrine's lesser buildings and walk beneath the gray granite span of the *torii* gate leading from the grounds.

When I was a young man, I used to tell my mother that I wanted to be a movie director and writer, a businessman artist. I had big dreams, or maybe I should say those were not big dreams but simply a lot of big talking.

I pass my hand affectionately over the headless neck of one of a pair of stone lion dogs that flank the gate, and remember the night I came here after successfully avoiding the sword that Masaaki Hatsumi had slammed down at the back of my waiting head. Headless even then, this same cold statue had seemed to mock in good humor the importance my own emotions had assigned to that final test. Head or no head, this silent guardian had seemed to say, I will persevere. Who is to lament what he calls my loss, when I myself am content with the knowledge that I am indeed a timeless spirit. No one, the headless lion dog had seemed to beam happily that night of another year, can take that away from me.

RH: The people who were able to attend our training seminars with you in the United States really enjoyed being with you and the other Japanese instructors. Now many Americans are trying to set it up so they can travel to Japan for training here. Many had the chance to see the art we have been offering for years from a new perspective, even though it was just a beginning glimpse.

MH: I think my own students have had to grow up, as well. I slept only two hours every day during that trip to America. I stayed up and wrote each night. I consciously worked at setting an example for the Japanese instructors who accompanied me. Every chance I got, I scolded them and surprised them and tried to keep them off balance. I wanted that trip to be training for their future when they may have to travel by themselves. I must be healthy, though. I never felt that I was tired.

RH: Perhaps that was due to your disciplined daily training.

MH: No, it's due to my daily fooling around. (Laughter.) But I am consistent even in my weaknesses. Even if I drink too much,

I make it a rule to take a walk like this at least one hour at the close of every day.

I would have to say that my worst habit, in a way, is my big ego. I think my wife has given up on me. But my ego is countered by the fact that I do not have any sense of how to handle money. When I went to America in 1982 on your invitation, that was the first time I had ever ridden first class on a plane. You bought me a first-class roundtrip ticket from Japan to Ohio, but I had no idea of how much money you had spent on me.

SKH: My teacher deserves only the best. First class is the only class.

MH: I got on the plane and I was on my way to America. I did not even know how much money our household had. This might be embarrassing to admit, but my wife does not even allow me to buy a train ticket. So my lifetime dream is to carry a lot of money around in a bag like the mailman, and go to luxurious spots and invite everyone to have a good time.

I do invest my money in collectible historical martial arts weapons. You know that I live in a shabby little dwelling. I don't even have a car. That's fine because when I feel that I have to purchase a particular tool, I can spend my money on that. My mother had bone cancer, and a lot of my money went toward her hospital bills. I knew I had to save some money to have a proper memorial service and funeral for her. I was not exactly what could be called a model son, so I wanted to do the best I could for her when she departed this world.

Before my mother died, she told me a wonderful story. When I was a young man, I used to tell my mother that I wanted to be a movie director and writer, a businessman artist. I had big dreams, or maybe I should say those were not big dreams but simply a lot of big talking. My mother's father, who was respected highly in his village, accused me of being a braggart, boasting of becoming this or that. But my mother said to me several times before her death that even though her father called me a braggart, "You became what you set out to become, so even a braggart can be a prophet."

I thought my mother was great. In educating a child, a mother's influence and power over the child is remarkable. There is a proverb, "*Mobo san sen no oshie,*" or, "The mother of Mo-shi [372–289 BC, Chinese Warring States era sage] moved three different times for the sake of her son's education."

I was given those words of praise by my mother before she departed. My mother had bone cancer, as I said. I avoided putting her in a big hospital because, as a doctor myself, I knew that in a large and impersonal institution they would simply cut her up piece by piece. I didn't feel comfortable with that idea, and I felt sorry for her. I hired a nurse for her and put her in a small private hospital that was run by a friend of mine. On the morning of my mother's death, my sister called me up and said that our mother was in critical condition and wanted me to come over right away, and also wanted me to contact our relatives. But I didn't inform my relatives of my mother's condition, because most of them were old, some had heart problems, some had palsey, and I did not want them going into shock.

I went to the hospital. When I got there, they put her on an oxygen respirator, and the doctor left the room saying that if there was any change, let him know. My mother said that her heart ached, so I massaged her for about an hour and a half. Then she was quiet. All of a sudden she said her chest hurt again. Her hands stiffened, and that was the end of her life.

Before that, my mother's breathing was irregular. My sister suggested that we should call the doctor, but I told her that it was not necessary. Instead, I told her to keep holding our mother's hand. I knew she was dead, and I called the doctor and he gave us the word that our mother was in fact dead. The nurse came in and they started to clean my mother's body while we waited there. But the nurse was so slow that I took her place and I did the job myself. I cleaned her and I dressed her. I had taken care of her for nine years while she was in the hospital. When you have done that for nine years, no tears fall from your eyes when it is finally over. I felt as though I had been involved in a big battle. I was relieved that the struggle was over.

Because of my commitment to a life in the martial arts, I never did anything evil or wrong-natured. Carrying on my work in my clinic, I never gave my mother any cause to worry about me. I never had to borrow money for her care. I was also able to establish the Bujinkan dojo network. Some people say that if my mother had not gone through this protracted illness, a Bujinkan *hombu* (central) *dojo* could have been established much sooner. But that is not a good way to think. Maybe next year the *hombu dojo* will be set up. With the money from books and other things, we will be able to build a *hombu dojo* and lodging place where Bujinkan people, true instructors, can stay while training here in Japan. We can set up a special room where you can stay, and call it the Hayes room. (Laughing.) I can see it now. This will become a historical site in the future. It could be on the route of sight-seeing tours in Japan. Stephen K. Hayes slept here.

SKH: Do my descendents get the admission ticket royalties from this shrine?

MH: (Laughing, and then a pause.) I do not have any children of my own, so I think that my inheritors will be the ones who carry on my thoughts. I would like to move Takamatsu-sensei's grave to this area so that I could create a Bujinkan's Mecca here. I feel that I will be able to do this soon. That is why I want my books to come out. This is from the bottom of my heart. I am not doing this for the sake of money, but because I want to build something that we can all share. I think this is important. We need to have a pilgrimage site, a *seichi* ("sacred spot").

RH: Yes, that is a very good idea to have a *hombu*. It would be much easier for our students and other foreigners to come here for training.

MH: I would like to have a translator at our headquarters, so that everything could be dealt with through me directly. If I leave it to my students, there would always be that buffer to possibly get in the way, a cushion that might allow for some misunderstanding. I think this is an important consideration. To avoid misunderstandings, everything should be handled directly through our headquarters.

RH: When new people come to us, they have some ideas about ninjutsu. They know that this art was born from a need for survival. Believing that ours is a really practical fighting system, they may still wonder about their own personal effectiveness in self-protection on the street. How do we teach the beginners to have confidence in themselves?

MH: First, the most important thing to do is to make them realize that it will take many, many years to develop the ability to defeat an adversary, if the student only concentrates on the details of technique.

RH: Make them realize?

MH: Yes, they must realize this. And then in their daily training, let them use their imagination to cultivate a proper attitude for what they would have to do if they were forced to fight against an attacker. If they cultivate this proper attitude, they can even handle some attack situations without the benefit of having many physical techniques in their repertoire. The student should not have to depend on techniques. Something that he perceives from the training will order him to avoid a dangerous situation when it arises. This kind of awareness is important to cultivate.

Let me tell you about *shinken gata* ["live blade technique," the real thing]. In the old days, Hayes-san, *musha shugyo* was the way to cultivate reliable warrior skills in Japan. When there was a war, could students attend training at a dojo every day? Of course not. Training halls themselves did not even exist. Teachers moved here and there as they were needed. You might have seldom seen your teacher, so when you did see him, you learned as much as you could from him in the short span of a few days. What you learned from him in that short time would give you some suggestions for improving physically, mentally, and technically. These training tips were at best suggestions, and in the real fighting world, these student warriors created their own survival methods based on these suggestions. These suggestions are what we later came to call the fundamentals. Based on their abilities to flesh out these fundamental principles, the students survived in the world of constant confrontation. [The converse is also significant; those who did not survive did not leave their obviously unsuitable techniques behind.] This process is so important to understand.

In *shinken gata*, learning new things is always important, but if you are not blessed with good luck, you will not survive. You will be killed, even though you might have acquired much knowledge through your studies. You could then ask, "Well then, what's the point of training, if it all comes down to luck?" Well, the truth is that there are no absolutes in the martial arts. Human life is the same. There is no absolute. Even though you regularly see a doctor for care and examination, when it is time for you to go, you go. There may be an accident, a disease like cancer. You never know about tomorrow. Since you never know what will happen tomorrow, it also makes it more enjoyable to look forward to tomorrow.

There is no one who wants to go into a fight with the sure knowledge that he will lose. But even I myself do not have any guarantee when it comes to winning or losing. You don't either. An attacker might just get in a lucky shot. Who knows? But when I enjoy myself, I am in control, even though I do not think about being in control.

This may be complicated, and I think that many instructors will find it difficult to understand what we are discussing right now. I know you understand this, Hayes-san, because you have gone through it all. Therefore, I felt like I wanted to bring this book out together with you. So I want beginners to read this book over and over again. Real fighting is an experience totally removed from what you go through in the training hall. You just cannot even imagine what it is like unless you've been there. It certainly is not like the things you see in the martial arts movies. Until you get to that point of actual combat involvement, you can never know. This is important to acknowledge.

SKH: In these days of relative civil peace, it is so easy for martial arts instructors to go on with all these theories about survival combat, even though they have never been there themselves. It is hard, if not impossible, for the student to judge the real from the illusion. With all these radically different styles of martial art available, it is so hard to tell which ones are truly reliable and which ones are useless.

MH: Therefore, one of my favorite slogans is, "*Saitei no kesaku,*" ["The lowest and yet a masterpiece."]. By this I mean that the techniques of our martial arts training are a starting point. There has to be some starting point for everything. I tell my students, looking at the techniques in my books, "These are my lowest techniques, my techniques for beginners. They're nothing."

I am not, however, telling them that those techniques themselves are insignificant things. The techniques are the starting point in the journey toward mastery. There is a starting point of a book, right? But when I tell the students that the books contain my lowest techniques, the students mistakenly think that the books do not mean much. So I have to remind them that each book is also a masterpiece. Those techniques are their starting point. As a student of the martial arts, there has to be a starting point. That is what I want to say.

SKH: Some people look at how you move now, and see your actions as being very light, dance-like, almost gentle. I believe that the reason you can move that way now is because you went through a lot of hard training, experiencing bruises here and there. That is the way you trained me, because that is the way Takamatsu-sensei trained you. Isn't that true?

MH: Yes, that's true. That's it. There is no other way.

SKH: But now, obviously, new students have no way to be able to see the training as it was in the past, how it was when I first became your student all those years ago. They attend one of my seminars where I emphasize the crucial importance of hard-hitting, realistic fighting skills as the only basis for advancement in ninjutsu training. They listen to my talk about survival combat, in all its grittiness. Then they watch the grace with which you move, and complain that I am not teaching the same art you are. They panic and go off on their own, leaving the Shadows of Iga Ninja Society to practice graceful movements without any foundation in combat-effective strikes and throws.

They do not understand that I emphasize grace and fluidity as

When you were living here in Japan as a student, I twisted your arms way too far, punched you too hard, and tore at you until you bled, but you endured it all and I salute you for that. But if you do that to new people now, they will not continue attending your seminars.

a result of advancing skills in the fundamentals, not as the place to begin. I mean, it took you many decades to get where you are today. It is ludicrous to assume that the students can learn to do what you can do in a year or two. "That's not the way Dr. Hatsumi moves," has become an almost universal whine uttered by my critics in the worldwide Bujinkan dojo network. They think that there seems to be a contradiction, but of course there is not. How do I explain this?

MH: The truth is that our students still have to go through the same kind of early training that you and I went through. They have to have a solid grounding in the basics. There is no way around that.

Personally, however, at my stage of development, I feel it is too much trouble to keep on doing all that hard-style training. Maybe people will not want to read that I let go of that kind of training because it was too much trouble, huh? In a way, I feel awkward putting it that way, but maybe some people will understand me. I will say again, however, that the truth is, to thoroughly learn this art, you have to go through the hard training first.

SKH: Certainly anyone with any brains will understand that you no longer choose to train with the rough-and-hard techniques of a raw beginner because you no longer require that crude level of power to be effective. I think that it is the same with development in any skill; the longer you continue to do something well, the less effort it requires. Tension and struggle are always the trademarks of the inexperienced.

MH: The problem is that nowadays, if you hurt your students through this hard training, the number of students training with you will dwindle down to very few. When you began your training with me, I didn't care at all about how many students we did or did not have.

SKH: I remember. In those days, there were only about eighteen of us training with you.

MH: At the same time, if you pour on the brutal and hard training today, you are at the mercy of all kinds of potential lawsuits. When you were living here in Japan as a student, I twisted your arms way too far, punched you too hard, and tore at you until you bled, but you endured it all and I salute you for that. But if you do that to new people now, they will not continue attending your seminars. You will have to close down your training hall.

RH: It is especially difficult in America, from the legal point of view.

SKH: America has the notorious reputation of being the land of the lawsuit. Of course, anyone going into a martial arts school ought to be intelligent enough to expect rough treatment, but the courts do not see it that way.

MH: Therefore, when I went to America, I respected your people, and I behaved with proper manners. Anyway, it is not your fault. These people who criticize you are only beginners, they are far junior to you in experience, so they do not know any better. I think that the significance of this book will be very great. You understand that, don't you?

RH: You really want us to print all this?

MH: Absolutely! Of course. That's why I wanted you to record this on tape. This is an important document in the history of our lineage. This book is intended to show the proper attitude for people who really want to get involved with our training. At the

When my students accuse me of lying to them or double-crossing them, I proudly tell them that I do that on purpose. I don't mean that I am actually a liar. I mean that I am merely employing an expedient method for getting across the truth of the martial arts.

same time, this is a teaching book that will help those already involved to better understand the Bujinkan training method. That's why it is necessary for you and me to talk like this.

I, as Toratsugu the tiger, am roaring!

SKH: Actually, it was probably easier for me in the beginning than it is for my students now. I was determined to get this training, no matter what was demanded of me. But I was studying with the grandmaster of the art, so I could figure that any seeming contradictions were there for a purpose. After all, I was studying with the world's only ninja grandmaster. It was easy to rely on faith and keep on going. My students, on the other hand, are required to have far more faith than I had—they are only studying with a student of the grandmaster. They could have all sorts of doubts when these seeming contradictions come up. It would be easy for them to wonder if in truth I might have misunderstood you somewhere along the way.

MH: Some people do not believe you, huh, Hayes-san, when you try to tell them that our modern training is based on hard training in the past? Tell them it was the same for me. I went through the same thing you did. Takamatsu-sensei's training was very thorough. Just looking at pictures of Takamatsu-sensei, you can imagine how hard our training was. Fingers attacked my ribs. Knees attacked my legs. It was just like a real fight, and that went on for fifteen years. After his death, for these past fifteen years, I have been contemplating [those previous fifteen years]. This past September 21st, I came to my answer.

In a way, it could be said that I was given this title of *soke* way in advance. Because of that fact, I know I caused you some difficulties, Hayes-san. But in the future I will try not to cause you so much trouble.

What I am telling you is the truth, and I do not consider this an embarrassing story for the world to hear. *Shugyosha*, "warriors on the path," do not win all the time. A martial artist, because he has experienced losing, will thereby know more about winning. Don't you think so?

There is no such thing as an absolute guarantee when it comes to winning and losing. One endeavors constantly, but he has no guarantee. It is the same with war. We were talking about war before. When you count the number of wars that have happened in the period of recorded human history, only one war was won because of correct strategy for every forty-seven wars that were won by means of deceit, trickery, lies, and double-crossing.

Therefore, when my students accuse me of lying to them or double-crossing them, I proudly tell them that I do that on purpose. I don't mean that I am actually a liar. I mean that I am merely employing an expedient method for getting across the truth of the martial arts. There is a proverb, *Uso mo hoben*, "Circumstances can justify falsehood," or maybe, "The end justifies the means."

The reason why I change from minute to minute is because if I do not do that, I will not be of any help to my students' growth. I have no concern at all with trying to control the Bujinkan dojo organization. I do this minute-to-minute changing because I want to be sure that my students grow as martial artists. Even when I make a promise, I only pretend that I will keep that promise. When I later choose not to keep the promise, my students get upset with me, accuse me of being a liar, and complain about the way I treat them.

SKH: I'd lose a lot of people if I employed those tactics. But then, as I said before, I am not the grandmaster. It's harder for my students to have faith in me.

MH: There are some people who get exasperated and leave the training because of my playing with truth and falsehood. But I can only remind you that these tactics are part of the advanced training that I offer my students. I do not make things up when I know that that falsehood will not help the student. I reverse the truth because I know that that is what he needs for his growth and for becoming a stronger person.

Even Shakyamuni the Buddha used this method. *Shaka mo hoben*, goes the proverb. ["Even the Buddha used the expedient."] In order to help a student become a better person, I will use lies. I employ this expedient means, and I can honestly say

that it is a part of my teaching program. I am not a mere conscienceless liar.

Look at the statistics on how many peace treaties have been kept in the history of the world. *Only one out of every 336 was honored.* Every other one was violated. Without knowing these facts, you cannot be a good mentor for sincere students going through *shinken gata.* These students must realize the truth about how human beings operate. That is a part of history. To make my students realize the meaning of history and the way to live, I break my word to them sometimes.

You know—I've done it to you many times.

SKH: I cannot deny that!

MH: I teach through my actions. I have to teach these lessons with my body in the world of experience. If you try to teach this art of ninjutsu from only the intellectual level, the students will never develop their true potential power. It will be theory alone. You cannot win the war on brains alone. Your whole being has to be used. This is important. Nowadays, people tend to judge everything from an intellectual point of view. But it should not be that way. Human beings are the ones who make things move.

The principal reason I am what I am now is because I used three times the normal amount of awareness getting here. I used three times the normal amount of financial investment to get what I have. It was also the same with three times the normal amount of physical endeavor. I had to invest three times the amount that normal people would be willing to invest. Even when I was seriously ill for five years, I never stopped training.

I was working for a living at the same time, too. I could barely see. I could barely stand. My students hit me. They threw me to the ground. But I kept going. I was not sure whether I would make it. In fact, I was so unsure of whether I would live or not, that for the first time, I made my students copy my *densho* training documents. Mysteriously enough, I survived.

At the time, I was betrayed by my best and most trusted friend. But the divine forces must have felt that I was needed in this world and kept me going. I trusted that friend, and even with his betrayal, I do not hate him. When I see him on the street, I greet him. The ninja philosophy includes, *Chijoku wo shinonde urami wo hoji saru*, or ["Endure the knowledge that you have been shamed, and do not hold onto hatred."] He could have shared what we have now. He could have been a part of all this. He may even feel that way too, possibly, but of course it is too late now.

I think that from now on the number of people who will leave the Bujinkan dojo will increase, to be perfectly honest. But that's fine. I am not a commercial teacher. You are not a *shonin*, or merchant, either, Hayes-san. You are a person who wants to follow the true path. You have been working to carry the truth of this art to the public. Therefore, I know you are truly a good person. I advise you to keep going.

It is fine if there are people who do not understand you and me. Those who do not understand cannot be forced into the light of understanding. It is important to acknowledge this reality.

At the same time, I feel compelled to reach out to offer this martial truth to those persons who are supposed to have it, to protect them and make them better persons. It will be that way for the rest of my life. But those who do not see that, or those who are too caught up in their own limiting egotistical views, will never feel accepted in the Bujinkan dojo. I can say this without hesitation. They decide by themselves and they quit by themselves and they disappear by themselves. This is because of their own personal qualities. My teacher used to tell me that those who do not share similar thoughts cannot be linked together.

SKH: To me, it is positively spooky to see the truth that no matter how much I may want some person to become truly powerful, there is no way in the world that I can motivate them to seek out that power if they secretly fear it or want to avoid it. I am truly amazed at the lengths to which some people will go to avoid having to give up comfortable weaknesses and take on new and

The scariness of ninjutsu is that you can end up trapping your own self through the very techniques of ninjutsu that you work to learn. That kind of person, the ones with the wrong motivations, disappear by themselves. It is scary how real this is. Those who are not needed will disappear.

unfamiliar powers. The more I work to force them to see, the more they resist. Some have actually ended up hating me because I went too far in forcing them to confront their own cherished limitations. I ended up becoming the bad guy in their minds, I am the thing to be gotten rid of, instead of that weakness that I tried to warn them of.

Many students have left me so that they could go off and indulge their weaknesses in the comfort of undisturbed pride. It is a good thing that I do not have to rely on teaching ninjutsu to support my family! The girls would have to be out on the streets selling pencils, I guess, with my approach to handling student "customers."

MH: What I think is important is captured by the great Iga ninja leader Momochi Sandayu's written comment, "Ninjutsu is not intended for the satisfaction of personal desires. The ninja employs his art because he is forced to protect his country, his leader, or his family. If you employ ninjutsu for the mere fulfillment of your own personal desires, your technique will be of no avail." This is an outstanding comment. We were saying before that some people get involved with this art because of personal needs for money or power. These desires or needs are of course a natural part of everyone. We all have them. They are not bad desires. But those who treat these needs as their number one priority will come to ruin. They will fade away.

SKH: I can attest to the cold hard fact that no matter how much I care, they will fade away if they are ultimately not destined to have this. It is amazing to me that the art still remains just as much a secret as it always has been, even though we are openly teaching the public. That has been a chilling, almost terrifying thing to realize. Willful ignorance will defeat any attempt made to enlighten it from outside. The will for enlightenment must come from within. I guess that it could be said that the art of ninjutsu, the lifeway of ninpo, is its own screening device, it seems.

MH: The scariness of ninjutsu is that you can end up trapping your own self through the very techniques of ninjutsu that you work to learn. That kind of person, the ones with the wrong motivations, will disappear by themselves. It is scary how real this is. Those who are not needed will disappear. Those who do not have that sufficient power of insight will disappear.

That quote I gave you is attributed to Iga ninjutsu *jonin* Momochi Sandayu from the Tensho era of the late 1500s. You yourself eventually began to carry those same feelings in your own heart, right? The two of you have become wonderful and outstanding *kaidensha* (fully realized and accomplished practitioners) because you could understand the feeling carried by Sandayu's words. You have obtained the *kuji no ho* power because you never gave up. You made it through all the hardships.

RH: I have a feeling that those hardships are not over yet.

MH: Oh, don't be pessimistic. After our book comes out, you can have yet one more reason to be more optimistic. Now that I am Toratsugu the tiger, I do not want my students to have to endure any more hardship. I feel that I have made it over the crest of the wave. We made it over the crest together, you and I. Everything will be fine from now on. I am not a weak *soke*. Since I am now called tiger, if I do not like something, I can just rip it to shreds and kill it if I need to. That's the truth. And my students are still trying to escape from me! (Laughing.) They say I used to become a tiger when I had too much to drink, and now they lament that I am a tiger when I am sober!

SKH: Keep on roaring, tiger. I love it, and the world sure can use it.

MARSHAL YOUR MARTIAL ARTS WITH THESE OTHER NINJUTSU BOOKS FROM CONTEMPORARY

Order
Quantity

_____ *Ninja Warrior: Bojutsu Defense Techniques* (4726-7)
by Jack Hoban
$7.95 FPT (paper)

_____ *The Mystic Arts of the Ninja: Hypnotism, Invisibility, and
Weaponry* (5343-7)   by Stephen K. Hayes
$8.95 FPT (paper)

_____ *Ninja Realms of Power: Spiritual Roots and Traditions of the
Shadow Warrior* (5334-8)   by Stephen K. Hayes
$7.95 FPT (paper)

_____ *Tantojutsu: A Ninja Defense Technique* (5095-0)
by Jack Hoban
$7.95 FPT (paper)

_____ *Tulka: A Tale of Modern Ninja* (5332-1)
by Stephen K. Hayes
$7.95 FPT (paper)

_____ *Wisdom from the Ninja Village of the Cold Moon*
(5383-6)   by Stephen K. Hayes
$8.95 FPT (paper)

_____ *Mind of the Ninja: Exploring the Inner Power*
(4951-0)   by Kirtland C. Peterson, Ph.D.
$11.95 FPT (paper)

Please enclose total payment plus $1.50 postage and handling for
the first book and $.75 for each additional book. Illinois residents
add 7% sales tax; California residents add 6%. Send check or money
order payable to Contemporary Books, or include VISA/MasterCard
number and expiration date.

Name _____

Address _____

City/State/Zip _____

☐ VISA ☐ MasterCard number _____

Expiration date _____

Signature _____

Please send your payment with this ad to:
Contemporary Books
Department NJA
180 North Michigan Avenue
Chicago, Illinois 60601

Allow six to eight weeks for delivery.   NJW1087